DUE DATE

Can We Know What's Right & Wrong?

ABSOLUTELY!

Carroll F. Hunt & Vicki Lake

Foreword by David A. Seamands

FRANCIS ASBURY PRESS
of Zondervan Publishing House
Grand Rapids, Michigan

Absolutely! Can We Know What's Right and Wrong?
Copyright © 1990 by Carroll F. Hunt and Vicki Lake

Francis Asbury Press is an imprint of Zondervan Publishing House,
1415 Lake Drive, S.E., Grand Rapids, Michigan 49506.

Library of Congress Cataloging in Publication Data

Hunt, Carroll Ferguson.
    Absolutely! : can we know what's right and wrong? / Carroll F. Hunt
and Vicki Lake.
    p.   cm.
    ISBN 0-310-51861-X
    1. Christian ethics–Popular works. I. Lake, Vicki. II. Title.
BJ1251.H86   1990
241–dc20   89-48418
                                                    CIP

All Scripture quotations, unless otherwise noted, are taken from the
HOLY BIBLE: NEW INTERNATIONAL VERSION (North American
Edition). Copyright © 1973, 1978, 1984, by the International Bible
Society. Used by permission of Zondervan Bible Publishers.

Edited by Robert D. Wood

Printed in the United States of America

90 91 92 93 94 95 / CH / 10 9 8 7 6 5 4 3 2 1

To our husbands
Charles Lake and Everett N. Hunt, Jr.
with gratitude for their patience
and enthusiasm for our project

contents

foreword

We live in a world of strange ethics. On the one hand are those who turn the Scriptures into a book of precise rules and regulations—do's and don'ts that cover every minute detail of life. These would absolutize the relatives of life.

On the other hand are those who deny any genuine authority to the Bible. They preach and practice a nebulous situation ethic and so relativize the absolutes.

In this book, Vicki Lake and Carroll Hunt, out of their rich pastoral and missionary experiences, do not fall into either error. They maintain the difficult but necessary balance of giving us the absolute guidelines of Jesus so that we will be able to make our own ethical decisions. From the heart of Christ's teachings in the heart of John's gospel, they extract eight central principles as basic for making Christian choices. They are absolutes in the sense that they are the foundation upon which we may safely and securely build our lives.

Adolph Rupp of the University of Kentucky was often called "the winningest coach in the history of basketball." Whenever his team lost a game or two he would call his players together and say, "All right now. Forget the fancy stuff. Let's get back to the basics." Then for several hours he would have them practice running, passing, dribbling, and shooting. This book is a clear call to get back to the basics. It is a good resource to put into the hands of an inquiring non-Christian who needs to understand the fundamental principles of the faith. It would also help the mature saint who needs a reminder of those foundation stones. *Absolutely!* will be of great value to beginner believers, who, in the midst of their newfound joy need to discover the basics that will sustain them long after the initial high emotions have lessened.

I can best commend this book to you in the words of Jesus: "This do and you will live"!

David A. Seamands
Professor of Pastoral Ministries
Asbury Theological Seminary
Wilmore, Kentucky

Introduction

Absolutes. Are there any?

One wonders. A recent *USA TODAY* article states that telling right from wrong is about as easy as nailing eggs to a barn door.

A New Age guru claims that "in the totality of beingness there is no absolute anything—no rights or wrongs, no higher or lower aspects. . . . Absolutes are concoctions of our rational minds."

Counseling professor, pastor, and author David Seamands says, "From Sesame Street to the university professor with his PH.D. we are taught there are no absolutes. We are floundering in a sea of relativism."

But Seamands goes on to say that the child of God can pattern his life after concepts taught by Jesus Christ, concepts relevant to citizens of the twenty-first century.

Author and pastor Charles Swindoll wrote in *Come Before Winter*, "Like a swamp of murky, slimy water, our society has either rethought, resisted, or completely rejected absolutes. Not the church! It still stands on the timeless bedrock of scripture."

Jesus came to our world straight from the heart of God with an armload of absolutes that offer security and resources. In John's gospel, chapters thirteen through fifteen alone contain a lifetime of imperatives spoken by the Master with clarity and simplicity. Through the pages of this little book let's look at a few chosen because they are basic and relevant, and because Jesus used them frequently. These concepts are foundation stones sturdy enough to bear the weight of all the other choices you are called upon to make. Whether you are a curious non-Christian, a new believer full of joy and wonder at discovering Jesus' love for you, or a seasoned follower of his who could use a refresher on the beauty of the basics, this book is for you. We offer you here absolutely the greatest imperatives ever given by God through Jesus Christ.

Don't be misled. Herein you'll find do's and be's at a different level perhaps than you are expecting. No mays or may-nots about liquor, sex, or interest rates. These are the anchors, however, that can hold you stable and secure in the sea of relativism that floods and threatens our world.

And speaking of "we," two of us are communicating together in these pages from our two sets of experiences. So when one of us is telling you a story, you'll see which one it is because her name, either Vicki or Carroll, will appear in parentheses early in the tale. We suggest that you read the Bible verses listed just below each chapter title. They'll help you understand what we're talking about and what we're basing our assertions on. In fact, keep a Bible handy as you read *Absolutely!* because almost every page holds reference to Scripture that illuminates the topic under discussion.

Now discover with us what Jesus has to say about absolutes. It all begins with what you decide to do when you invite him into your life.

1
believe

Read John 14:1–11
Key Verses: John 14:6, 11

I (VICKI) WAS CONFUSED and slightly frightened. Where was I? I didn't know.

During our visit to colonial Williamsburg in Virginia, my husband and two daughters coaxed me to tackle the garden maze planted by the governor to entertain his guests. Even mazes on paper frustrate me. Here with the governor's tall 200-year-old shrubs closing in around me, I realized all over again I did not like mazes, even though this one was supposed to be fun.

The trouble with mazes is that they're designed with only one way to the goal. You can't unstop dead ends. You can't bridge barriers. You can't even decide that the end of one of the stopped-up channels is where you want to be after all. One way alone leads to the pre-set goal.

To many people, life is a maze of wrong turns, frustration, and searching. Jesus' disciples, twelve men who'd lived with and learned from him, experienced extreme frustration during their last night with their Master before his death. Three profound questions emerged from the pain and confusion of those final moments together, questions with which we can identify. As we listen to Jesus' responses to his friends' questions, we will find his way through the mazes of our lives.

Jesus knew the turning point had come. His three years of public ministry, his time to live with these twelve men, his opportunities to teach them to know God via his human presence—all were finished. As Son of God, the work he came to do was almost complete and soon he would leave.

With this knowledge bearing in upon him, Jesus rose from the table around which they would eat a final meal together. He shrugged out of his street clothes, scooped up a towel and knotted it about his waist. Conversation probably died away as the men watched their Master splash water into a basin and stoop in front of Peter.

"Lord! Are you going to wash my feet?" Maybe Peter pushed away the hand that reached for his knobby, calloused feet as he gaped at the kneeling Jesus.

"You don't understand right now what I'm doing," Jesus replied, "but later you will understand."

"No!" Peter almost shouted in disbelief and embarrassment. "You shall never wash my feet!"

Jesus was communicating final truths to his disciples. They knew they faced change, although they couldn't know how the next few days would alter human history.

Jesus explained what was coming, preparing the

twelve for the leadership roles that awaited them. He knew they were confused by what they heard him say. He was telling them it was the end of the road. Of course they were frightened. Jesus die? What then? Will I die in the coming turmoil, too? Even if I don't, what will become of me after he's gone?

Jesus knew their thoughts and their hearts as always, so he began with comfort. "Don't let your hearts be troubled. Trust in God; trust also in me . . . I am going . . . to prepare a place for you . . . I will come back and take you to be with me . . . You know the way to the place where I am going."

Thomas, one of the twelve, blurted out his pain and confusion in denial, which was really a question: *"Lord, we don't know where you are going."* In his willingness to verbalize the fears of his fellow disciples, Thomas represents us all. He was asking, "Where are you going?" Inherent in his question are more profound ones: "What is life all about?" "What happens when you (or we) die?" It sounded as if Jesus were promising life after death. Can we believe him?

A father, riding home from his wife's funeral, wanted to tell his children they could. Devastated by their mother's death, the children's pain was breaking his heart. He cast about for a way to make them understand that a Christian's life doesn't end with death. Just then a huge truck pulled alongside their car, its bulk obliterating the sunshine as it passed.

"Children, which would you choose, to be run over by that truck or to be run over by its shadow?"

Puzzled by such a dumb question, the children replied, "Well, sure, the shadow, of course."

"Well, that's what happened to Mommy. Because

she is a Christian and had trusted Jesus as her Savior, she's gone to heaven. Her death is only the touch of the shadow. She's not lost forever; she's with the Lord."

Important in Jesus' response to Thomas is that he has gone on ahead of us and confronted death. He prepared the way for us. In Hebrews 6:20 Jesus, it says, went before us. The King James Version calls him the "forerunner." To people in those days that word meant a reconnaissance group that preceded the Roman army into an area or situation. They checked out the sector, insuring safety for the bulk of the army. Jesus reconnoiters our path to guarantee our safety and well-being. We encounter nothing he doesn't already know about.

Another use of the same word had to do with the port of Alexandria, which was treacherous for large ships. Small pilot boats, forerunners, met the ships and guided them through the channels and past the rocks until they docked safely. Jesus, as our forerunner, endured death at Calvary, then moved on before us into heaven to prepare a place so that where he is, we can also be.

Thomas' query had another part, which is our second question. Jesus had said, "You know the way to the place I'm going." Thomas disagreed.

"How can we know the way?" he asked. And so do we.

Jesus died for us. He rose from the grave and went ahead of us into heaven so that we could join him there. But let's get practical. Even if we believe that he's done all this, how can we know the way to follow him?

"I," Jesus answered Thomas, and us, "am the

way, the truth, and the life. No one comes to the Father except through me."

Many years ago in Korea people seldom saw motor vehicles driving through their little farming and fishing villages. Ox carts and an occasional bus were common, but most Koreans walked to wherever they wanted to go. So when a Land Rover-driving missionary like my (Carroll's) husband would roar up to a crossroad in a flurry of dust, anxious to know the way to the next town, he'd ask directions in his best language-school Korean from a farmer grazing his ox at the roadside. The conversation often went like this:

Missionary: May I ask you a question?
Farmer: What? (*Is this person really speaking my language?*)
Missionary: (Louder) I want to ask you a question!
Farmer: Oh, oh. Yes. (*I never saw such funny-colored eyes.*)
Missionary: Is this the road to Kongju?
Farmer: To where? (*Why's he going to Kongju?*)
Missionary: To Kongju. I'm going to Kongju.

The farmer would then pause, draw breath through his teeth with a hiss, and stare off into the distance. He knew both roads eventually reached Kongju and that the one to the right was shorter. But he also knew that buses used only the one to the left because the right fork had a bridge out and the river was up, thanks to heavy rains.

But do green-eyed foreigners who rush about in Land Rovers need bridges? And how can I answer, he wonders, when I don't know what this person wants to hear. Can he understand me if I do answer?

A dismaying method of finding one's way any-
where, don't you agree?

On the other hand, happy was my husband when
approaching a crossroad to find a young man in a
white shirt waiting under a tree. He'd flag down the
vehicle and jump in, saying, "I've come out from the
Kongju church to show you the way. Please turn left
here."

With such a prepared guide, finding the way
becomes a relationship in following a leader instead
of an exercise in isolated fumbling.

Several years ago my husband and I (Vicki) were
sent to Australia for a six-week speaking tour by
OMS International, the missionary organization of
which we were a part. Charles did most of the
speaking, but our president informed me that when
we left Australia Charles would fly to New Zealand's
South Island for ministry and I to North Island for a
separate assignment.

I was uneasy. "But I don't know a single soul in
New Zealand. I've never been there before," I
thought. Realizing my silent anxiety, our leader
spoke gently. "Now, Vicki, your itinerary has been
planned. You will fly from Sydney to Auckland to
Mount Maunganui. There you will be greeted by a
woman named Marion Clare who will provide lodg-
ing and transportation to all your meetings. Don't
worry about anything."

As the little plane circled Mount Maunganui, I
searched for signs of Marion Clare. Several gave me a
warm New Zealand welcome but I was relieved to
hear, "I am Marion Clare and I will be your hostess
while you are in New Zealand." She's still my loving

New Zealand mom, and God, who knows the maze of this life, always provides the perfect guide.

What comfort to be shown the way, which is what Jesus does for us. And he not only *shows* us the way, he *is* the way.

"I am the way," he said. Without him there's no going.

"I am also the truth." Without him there's no knowing.

"And I am the life." Without him there's no living.

In that verse nestle some of the Bible's most beautiful words. "No one comes to the Father except through me." According to this, there's only one way to God. Jesus is the way, the truth, the life. An absolute.

"Jesus is the way," someone said, "in order that the human will may choose it. He is the truth in order that the mind may comprehend it. He is the life in order that the human heart may experience it. No one forces us to choose the correct way. We're created with free wills, endowed with ability by our Creator to make good and bad choices without coercion.

I (Vicki) remember tucking in our younger daughter Kara, who had crawled into bed a half-hour early as punishment for disobeying me. She was tired, frustrated, and upset at losing her playtime.

"Mommy, why does God make me do all these bad things?" she asked.

"Honey, God didn't make you be naughty," I protested.

"He knows everything!" she argued. "He knows what I'm gonna do."

"You can't blame God for this," I said. "You have the right to choose whether you do right or wrong."

She shook her curly head in disgust. "I was afraid you were gonna say that."

God never forces himself upon us even though he gave us the best he has, his Son Jesus, who died to provide the way, the only way to the Father.

Philip, who appears to have thought it all through, had another question for Jesus; a demand, really. He said in effect, "All right, if no one can come to the Father except by you . . . then you show us God. *Show us the Father.*"

Maybe you've wanted to demand something similar. "If I could only see God, then I could understand. If I could only know he's involved in this situation, I'd feel better. If only I knew that he is in the maze with me. Could someone please show me God?"

Jesus responded to Philip's need . . . and ours. "Don't you know me, Philip? . . . Anyone who has seen me has seen the Father . . . Don't you believe that I am in the Father, and that the Father is in me? The words I say to you are not just my own. Rather, it is the Father, living in me . . . Believe me when I say that I am in the Father and the Father is in me; or at least believe on the evidence of the miracles themselves."

Believe me, Jesus urged. To believe. What does it mean? The dictionary defines it thus: "To have confidence in the truth or the reliability of something without absolute proof." Believe, in the Bible, is the verb form of the noun *faith*. *Believe* is used more than 240 times in the New Testament; more than 90 times in John's gospel alone. When Jesus asks us to believe him, simply to *trust* him, he offers proof of the authenticity of his claim.

"If you can't yet believe that I'm in the Father and the Father is in me, then look at what I did." He reminded Philip and his friends of the miracles and other events of the three years they had spent together. "Believe my words," he said, "and believe my works."

A verse in Hebrews backs up Jesus' claim. "The Son is the radiance of God's glory and the exact representation of his being" (1:3). Think about what these words tell us. God, through his Son, came to earth—not as king, not into wealth or privilege. He came as a squalling, helpless newborn in a carpenter's home, "an exact representation of [God's] being." God, through his Son, worked, sweat, and probably tore open blisters on his hands. He may even have mashed his thumb with a wild hammer blow or two. When you're scrubbing floors, immersed in the office or machine shop routine, or waiting for your carpool ride, remember that God worked, too.

He not only worked, he confronted temptation. Hebrews also tells us that he was tempted just as we are, but without sin (4:15–16). So he was born, worked, faced temptation, and then was executed by the same cruel method used for criminals. But he strode out of his borrowed tomb in victory over death and returned to heaven, his incarnation of God's great love complete at last.

That's the answer! This is where we're headed.

We can follow him into the same glory if we choose the right path through life's maze, if we believe in him as Savior. Simple and familiar?

Certainly. Many of us have heard some version of this all of our lives.

Profound? Humbling? Without question. Ponder what God did for us because he loved us so much, then see what happens inside you. Reverence, awe, and wonder well up whenever we consider the Father's matchless plan. He sent his only Son, Jesus Christ, and whoever of us believes on him will not perish. Neither do we have to stumble along through wrong turns and confusion. We can have eternal life. We can know him who is the way.

Jesus answers our questions about life, about what path we should take, and how we can know God. All *we* have to do is believe in him.

* * *

God, thank you for your absolutes that can hold me safe as I pick my way through the mazes of my life. Thank you for belief, for faith. Make mine strong. Cultivate it, nourish it, and protect it. Teach me more about yourself, for Jesus' sake.

What Do You Think?

1. Think about a time when you were lost and couldn't find your way. What lessons did you learn in the midst of your confusion? How can you identify with the disciples' feelings in John 14:1–11?

2. How did Jesus' words comfort the disciples? How do they comfort you?

3. What absolute is given in John 14:6?

4. How has Jesus become your truth, your life, and your way?

5. According to John 14:1–11, how can you truly know God? How does he reveal himself?

2
ask

Read John 14:12–14

I (CARROLL) HAD NEVER needed help so badly in my life. That wretched letter lay on the floor where I'd thrown it, but I couldn't see it through my tears. The university said no again, and it looked as if my middle-aged student husband would never attain his crucial career goal of earning his PH.D. What would become of us? How could he teach without proper credentials? And how could God let us crawl out on this limb and then watch while an academic committee sawed it off?

My husband, Ev, was out of town, of course; he is regularly when crises arise. So I ranted and wept around the house, alone with my pain, anger, and fear. Maybe it's hard to understand why I was so upset, but we'd staked our whole career, it seemed to me at the time, on this degree and had given several stress-filled years to acquiring it. So right or wrong, another rejection of his dissertation devastated me beyond reason.

I sat on the floor and shook my fist at the ceiling. "Where are you?" I shouted at God. "Do you care what's happening to us? If you do, show me now!"

The phone rang. I stumbled over to answer it. "Hello?"

"Carroll? What's wrong?" My special friend Kay sensed something was badly out of whack with me.

"Oh, Kay, are you my answer?" I blubbered.

"I'll be there in ten minutes."

She hung up and dashed over to me, and I knew that God was there, that he cared about me. In desperation I asked him for help and he gave it. Kay came and sat with me and listened to my woes. She brought perfect understanding because her husband is also a man of books and papers, so she knew well what this meant to us.

Of course sanity returned at last. The reluctant degree came round and Ev has plenty of classrooms open to him. It is hard to re-create the desperate emotions of that day, but one part of it I'll never forget; I asked God for help—and he gave it.

To ask God for something is to pray. We human beings seem to carry a built-in instinct to ask help from higher powers. People of most cultures employ methods that they hope will evoke response from the gods or powers they honor. Buddhists expect the rising blue smoke from burning incense to bear aloft their wishes. Muslims bow toward Mecca several times each day to beseech Allah's aid. Primitive people pay shamans to placate the spirits and ease their ills.

What did Jesus say about prayer? He speaks of it

in John 14 as an integral part of what we, his followers, are to be and do.

"Anyone who has faith in me will do what I have been doing. He will do even greater things than these, because I am going to the Father. And I will do whatever you ask in my name, so that the Son may bring glory to the Father. You may ask me for anything in my name, and I will do it" (vv. 12–14).

Jesus tells us to ask him and he will respond, an unequivocal promise, an absolute. Can it be trusted?

Yes, it can because Jesus doesn't lie, and the belief we talked about in the last chapter enters in. When we choose to believe in Jesus, we accept his promises as true and reliable.

But do you struggle with the idea of getting something for nothing? Does asking make you think of God as the big candy machine in the sky?

Don't worry, God is never manipulated, although we try. He loves us, he worked out a costly plan to save us, and he wants to give us what we need. Jesus forged a bridge from God to us so we can communicate with our Creator. As soon as we cross this bridge we can bring our petitions to him. The bridge must be crossed, though. Belief in and acceptance of Jesus Christ as Savior is the first condition to asking.

Conditions for Prayer

Conditions? Yes, they're there. They keep the asking from becoming a nonchalant push on the gratification button. They are guidelines that align our asking with the character and purposes of God. Conditions restrict, limit, or modify circumstances, says the dictionary. Let's consider God's conditions that affect our asking.

In John 14:12, Jesus says that "anyone who has faith in me" can pray. God cannot respond to the prayers of one who doesn't believe in him unless that prayer is to ask for faith and redemption through Jesus.

Then he goes on in verse 14 to say, "You may ask me for anything in my name, and I will do it." In my name. Have you ever needed a co-signer to complete a business deal? He may have meant the difference between success and failure for you. Or did someone ever give you a signed blank check and tell you to buy what you needed? To pray in Jesus' name means we're not alone in this; he endorses our right to ask.

But that's not all. Praying in Jesus' name gives us *perspective*. It moves us out of ourselves and into him. Consider his prayer in the Garden of Gethsemane as he confronted the approaching agony of the cross. He asked God to let that bitter cup, that awful experience, pass him by—but if not, he went on, "then your will be done."

To pray with Jesus' perspective means to pray "your will be done" and to know that what we ask for lines up with God's plan for us. To reach this point requires that we stand close to him so we can learn to align our goals with his.

Also, praying in Jesus' name means that we don't have to appear before God besmirched by our failures and faults. No, we go in Jesus' name, the perfect one, who has forgiven our sins and failures. We're covered by his *perfection*.

Teamed with perspective and perfection is *power*. Being allowed to use his name makes available to us

Christ's strength and power. Miracles and the bold speaking out in Jesus' name by the disciples after his return to heaven show us how he makes his power available to his followers. Read Acts 3 and 4 and discover the power of the name of Jesus.

When and where can we pray? There are no limitations. We can ask anything in his name, we've learned. Also, we can ask it wherever and whenever we need to. When Jesus was crucified, the curtain in the temple at Jerusalem, which separated the people from the holiest place and which sheltered God's presence, was torn in two, showing the world that because of his sacrifice we can now approach God. The important test is whether we know deep down we can ask God for something with Jesus' name as our endorsement, knowing that the granting of what we ask will honor the Father and not just gratify us. That's Jesus' goal and we must align ourselves with it, adopting his purposes as our own.

Other conditions pop up in the Bible. Read Matthew 21:21–22. "If you believe, you will receive whatever you ask for in prayer." Absolutely simple and straightforward—yet difficult to trust. Children are best at this, it seems. Like my (Vicki's) friend's little girl who was saddened because her puppy was hurt.

"I'm gonna pray for him right now," she announced. Eyes squeezed shut, she informed her Lord about the problem that troubled her. Then her eyes popped open and she declared with an airy wave of her hand, "He'll be OK."

Of course adult life contains more complex problems and needs than an injured puppy, but belief is still just that and is crucial to our developing relationship with Jesus Christ. We must believe that God can and will listen when we pray.

A further condition appears in 1 John 5:14–15. It says in part, "If we ask anything according to his will, he hears us." Praying is not forcing our will upon God, but rather discovering his will for every situation.

Stand again in the garden's shadows and learn from Jesus at prayer. With painful honesty he asked his Father to allow him to bypass the agony which confronted him. But his understanding of prayer's conditions required him to say, "Nevertheless, not my will but yours be done." He submerged his desire into the Father's plan and found courage to look beyond the Cross to the Resurrection, beyond pain to the purpose of his death, which is why he could submit his preference to the Father's plan.

Praying in God's will isn't easy. Neither is persistence, but it is recommended when we're asking God for something. Luke 11:5–10 illustrates this in a practical way. Let's set that story in our day:

Unexpected guests arrive at the Smiths late one evening. Tomorrow is market day so the cupboards are empty. Mr. Smith slips out back and runs next door to the Joneses to borrow bread. Mr. Jones, already under the covers and snoring, hears Smith pounding on the back door.

"Ah, go 'way," he mumbles. "We're all asleep."

But Smith doesn't give up. The threat of hungry guests and his waiting wife keep him knocking. Finally, Jones stumbles downstairs and hands out bread to his neighbor.

"Ask and it will be given to you; seek and you will

find; knock and the door will be opened to you," was Jesus' summary of this story. Persist, he tells us.

Choosing between persistence and acceptance requires perception and spiritual sensitivity. For example, you pray for someone you care about to be healed, but he doesn't get better. Do you stop praying since it doesn't seem to be working? After all, if he dies he'll know perfect health in heaven. How do you know how long to persist? When to quit? What God's will is for the ailing one?

We suggest you persist in prayer until peace replaces anxiety. So long as the urgency, the burden to pray remains with you, then pray. But when release comes, when a comforting sense of well-being about the situation floods in and you feel that everything will be all right, then it is time for persistence to give way to acknowledgment that God's plan is working, whether his answer is yes or no.

Of course, if you're asking that someone accept Christ as Savior, you should persist for as long as it takes. This is God's will for everyone, Scripture tells us, so prayer for anyone's salvation is something we should pursue without giving up.

I (Vicki) remember when I was a small child that my mother prayed persistently for her aunt's salvation. Years passed before Aunt Evelyn accepted Christ, but in the meantime I often heard Mother say, "Aunt Evelyn will make a great Christian." She was right. When Aunt Evelyn decided to make Jesus lord of her life, she became an active worker and representative for him. As I sat at her funeral and listened to the accounts of how she influenced others toward God through her years of battling cancer, I thanked the Lord for a mother who persisted in prayer.

The Bible further tells us to pray with clean hearts. "If our hearts do not condemn us," it says, "we have confidence before God and receive from him anything we ask, because we obey his commands and do what pleases him" (1 John 3:21–22).

Remember when you were a child? Before you could get near the dinner table your mother would sing out, "Wash your hands!" If she was like ours, she checked them, front and back, before you were allowed to attack the fried chicken.

1 John 1:9 says, "If we confess our sins, he is faithful and just to forgive us our sins and to cleanse us from all unrighteousness" (KJV). Hearts washed clean by confession and forgiveness are a condition for asking of God.

One evidence of heart cleanness is our forgiveness of others. In Mark 11:24 Jesus tells us again that we can ask for whatever we want in prayer. He goes on in verse 25 to say, "And when you stand praying, if you hold anything against anyone, forgive him, so that your Father in heaven may forgive you your sins."

If we harbor bitterness or an unforgiving spirit even against unjust treatment, we can't expect God to respond to our asking. Just recently I (Vicki) knew I wasn't growing spiritually. During my quiet time I cautiously asked the Lord to show me why. All I could see through my tears as I stared at the pages of my Bible was a friend's name, someone toward whom I was bitter because of sin in his life, sin that had deeply affected one of my best friends. I knew I had to call and ask his forgiveness for my anger against him in order to gain the freedom of spirit I longed for. It was a difficult assignment, yet peace flooded my soul as we talked. Jesus set the example of forgiveness and he expects us to follow it.

God also expects us to pray with unselfish motives. An old man with more dollars than sense once wandered the world on Christian tours. He apparently bore a deep-seated dislike for certain branches of Christianity. When the tour bus passed churches on his blacklist, he'd point his bony finger and shout, "Curse it, Lord! Burn it down!" He seemed to expect the Lord to concur with his prejudices and hates.

In James 4:3 it says in part, "When you ask, you do not receive, because you ask with wrong motives." Maybe you don't want God to burn churches you don't like, but do you urge him to provide you with a more elegant home, promotion at work, or academic success for your child? There's nothing wrong with any of these *per se*, but you need to turn over these desires and look underneath. Why do you want them? To impress friends? To acquire more things? To satisfy your ego?

The rest of that verse in James says, in defining wrong motives, "that you may spend what you get on your pleasures." Check your motivation for each prayer request. Asking for someone's salvation or physical healing is certainly unselfish. So is praying for people in Christian ministry. But we need to test our motives about those things we request for ourselves and those we love. Ask the Lord to check them with you; it might change how and for what you pray.

Comfort in Prayer

"I don't even know how to pray about this!"

Have you come up against that wall yet? Do you face a situation so complex that good and bad, best and worst are blurred beyond recognition?

I (Vicki) experienced this dilemma as my mother lay critically ill with complications from pancreatitis. She'd already undergone three major surgeries. Innumerable times over the previous two months she'd stood at death's door. As I walked into her room in the intensive care unit one day, I discovered that she no longer recognized me and was tied to her bed with restraining belts. It broke my heart when she accused me of trying to poison her.

An experimental pain drug apparently had pushed her over the edge of reason. In anguish I ran from her room straight to the hospital chapel. I didn't know how to pray. Did I want her healed? Or set free to go to heaven? All I could do was claim what the apostle Paul wrote to the Romans. He said that the Holy Spirit would help me express myself when I didn't know how.

Listen to what he says. "The Spirit helps us in our weakness. We do not know what we ought to pray for, but the Spirit himself intercedes for us with groans that words cannot express. And he who searches our hearts knows the mind of the Spirit, because the Spirit intercedes for the saints [that's who we are] in accordance with God's will" (Rom. 8:26–27).

The Spirit Paul talks about here is the Holy Spirit, the Comforter who, Jesus promised, would remain with us, giving us spiritual power and peace even though Jesus returned to his Father in heaven. So the

Comforter enters into the process when we're under a prayer burden too heavy to bear alone. Even though we don't know what to ask for, the Spirit speaks on our behalf with intense communication groans, the Bible says, that go beyond normal words.

This is truth to believe in, assurance to hold onto in dark and difficult times, knowledge that there is a way through confusion and conflict. Best of all, it is further proof that God loves us more than we know. First he sent Jesus to redeem us, then the Comforter to sustain and enable us through life's rough spots.

But what happens when God says no? The apostle Paul faced this one. According to 2 Corinthians 12:7–10, he had a problem, something he called "a thorn in my flesh, a messenger of Satan, to torment me." No one knows what Paul's problem was, although speculation ranges from epilepsy to a difficult mother-in-law! Three times Paul asked God to take away this thorn, but so far as we know he never did. Instead, God responded this way: "My grace is sufficient for you, for my power is made perfect in weakness" (v. 9).

So Paul learned to boast in weakness since it was a means of honoring God by focusing on his strength instead of Paul's. He delighted in his affliction along with the insults, hardships, persecution, and difficulties that came his way. "For when I am weak," he wrote, "then I am strong."

This strength was not Paul's. Strength comes from God and was evident in Paul's weakness. And out of Paul's God-glorifying weakness came a major portion of the Bible, his letters to churches and groups of believers, which were inspired and preserved by the Holy Spirit. Some weakness!

It boils down to this: Are we victims or victors? Bitter or better? Even when God says no? What Christians have long called unanswered prayer is really a response different from the one we want, isn't it? But in the throes of having to endure situations we'd like to change, opportunity awaits to honor the Lord.

Challenges for Prayer

If you're not sure how to approach God in prayer, how to ask him for what you need and want, we suggest some methods to organize your thinking and your asking. These simple, practical acronymns can guide you.

The first one spells *acts*, acts of prayer. We include Scriptures for you that reinforce the importance of each phase of prayer.

A — Adoration. When we first approach God in prayer we should adore him, concentrate on how wonderful he is. Praise him for who he is (See 1 Chron. 29:11 and Ps. 145:1–6).

C — Confession. So you can come before the Lord with a clean heart, confess to him those sins you know you've committed but have not confessed. Admit your guilt and ask him to forgive you (1 John 1:9 and Ps. 32:5).

T — Thanksgiving. Thank God for all he's done for you. In Philippians 4:6 and 7, the Living Bible tells us to bring our requests to God and reminds us, "don't forget to thank him" (Eph. 5:20 and Ps. 100:4).

S — Supplication. This means bringing our petitions, our requests to God; praying for others as well as ourselves (Matt. 7:7 and James 4:2).

Another help for our praying comes from Jill Briscoe's book on prayer called *Hush, Hush*. She suggests an acronym that spells *praise*. First we need to *prepare*, not only our hearts but a place to be quiet and pray. I (Vicki) have a corner in my basement away from the traffic and turmoil of our home. It's not plush but is pleasing for spending time alone with my Lord. Then there's the woman in a group I discipled who said she took her Bible and notebook to the bathtub for her quiet time.

"But don't your things get wet?" we queried her.

"Oh, no," she laughed. "The tub is dry, and I even take a pillow and quilt for comfort. You see, no one bothers me when I'm in the bathroom."

Remember or *reflect* for a moment on all the things the Lord has done for you.

Adore him. Tell him you love him.

Imagine. Be creative and use your imagination in your talks with the Father.

Sing. Use a hymnbook and hum, warble, or whatever your musical skills allow, but praise him and even ask him for what you want through the medium of song. To him it's beautiful. Some of my (Vicki's) best quiet times have come when I've used a hymnbook. Once I decided to study songs with the theme of God's love. I rediscovered "The love of God is greater far / Than tongue or pen can ever tell," and "O the deep, deep love of Jesus, / Vast, unmeasured, boundless, free." And they brought tears to my eyes as I pondered the expanse of God's love. Then I turned to "Share His Love," which reminded me to give that love rather than selfishly keep it to myself.

Express your feelings, your concerns for yourself and others.

Another way to increase the power of your praying is to do it in partnership with someone else. Meet regularly and pray together. You'll discover not only growing prayer power within yourself but deepening love and spiritual commitment between you and your partner.

Sharla has been my (Vicki's) prayer partner for several years and we have seen some wonderful responses to our asking. We prayed her children through junior and senior high school. Now we pray for them in college. Just the other day I prayed while her daughter Holly was taking a business law exam. We prayed my children through the toddler years and into elementary and middle school. We prayed through the building project for her husband's orthodontics practice. I wouldn't trade this partnership for anything.

Keeping a prayer list or a journal reinforces your commitment to prayer as you watch the answers pile up. Some are years in coming, others are on the way before you ask. Keep track on paper how God responds to you. Browsing through the pages will strengthen your faith and cause you to relish God's goodness as you review his responses.

A photo album can be a family project. Collect pictures of people for whom you pray; missionaries and others in ministry, family members who need something special from God, and friends who've asked you to pray for them. Alphabetize the people in the photos and do all the A's one day, the B's the next, and so on. Little children can't read prayer lists but they love pictures and can learn early to ask God to help people they know.

Another family project could be to ask each

member to think of blessings and write them on slips of paper. Then during family prayers let one person draw out a blessing and read it to the family, an intimate reminder of God's love and willingness to listen when we pray. The same method works for prayer needs. Watch competitive little siblings learn to care as they pray about each other's problems.

Take a day of prayer alone. Sounds difficult, doesn't it? And it is. But if you plan ahead, maybe amplifying some of the acronyms we've already discussed, you can enjoy and profit from a private mini-retreat.

Whether you use some, all, or none of these suggestions, the crucial issue is that you pray. Prayer results in growing rapport between you and God, just as an interchange of selves promotes friendships between human beings.

Prayer is like a muscle. It develops and strengthens with exercise, so use it, test it, stretch it until you learn the truth of what Jesus told his friends. "Everything is possible to the man who believes."

* * *

Lord Jesus, you told a couple of blind men who wanted to see that according to their faith it would be done to them. My first asking of you is that you stretch and strengthen my faith.

What Do You Think?

1. In John 14:12–14, what reason does Jesus give for the disciples being able to do the works that he did? See also John 16:7.

2. What restriction does Jesus place on prayer in John 14:13–14?

3. What does James 4:3 have to say regarding prayer? What have been some of your recent motives in praying?

4. What lessons can you learn from Jesus' prayers in the Garden of Gethsemane? (Matt. 26:36–46)

5. Alan Redpath, a prominent preacher/teacher, once said, "I can't pray 'thy kingdom come' until I pray 'my kingdom go'." How does that relate to conditions for prayer?

3

trust

Read John 14:1–27 and
1 Kings 17:1–16

I (CARROLL) STOOD THERE for more than an hour. Watching Tokyo traffic is a fascinating pastime so I was not bored, just tired of standing in one place. But Ev and Kemp, my husband and our friend, said they would meet me in front of the souvenir shop at 4 P.M. So I waited.

Tokyo is not my town. I don't know the train system well enough to use it on my own. I don't speak Japanese so I couldn't jump into a taxi and go home. Neither can Ev, but he had an advantage; he was with Kemp who lived in Tokyo and can do all those things. Did they forget and go home without me? Funny I didn't worry more. I guess I figured that if they did, they'd just have to turn around and come back.

5:45 P.M. No sheepish Caucasian grins in the sea of Japanese politeness, no guys to take me home. I stood on my weary, aching feet rooted to the cement,

43

unable to take action and thereby forced to trust that those two tardy men would come.

Trust is one of God's absolutes. In order to understand his concept of trust, however, we must talk about anxiety or lack of trust. Our world overflows with anxious people as it hurtles toward the twenty-first century. Conventional wisdom has it that women are the major victims of stress, worry, and anxiety, but within a six-month period I (Carroll) listened to a significant number of stories about middle-aged men's stress-related trips to the emergency room or their search for ways to deal with anxiety overload. Both sexes are afflicted and it is endemic to our era.

We don't know how much money is spent each year to alleviate stress, anxiety, and worry. We do know that half of all hospital beds are filled with patients whose conditions were caused by nervous or mental troubles. We also know anxiety contributes to heart disease, high blood pressure, ulcers, and even arthritis. One doctor asserts that his practice would halve if people didn't worry.

My (Vicki's) brother, who is a medical doctor in family practice, once told me that he was considering hiring a counselor on his staff to deal with people's anxieties, which, he feels, cause many of his patients' physical problems.

To top it off, the word *worry* comes to us from the distant mists of Anglo-Saxon English. Its old form was *wyrgan*, and it meant in those days *to strangle*. Maybe you feel strangled at times by worry.

Causes for Worry

In John 14 Jesus' friends worried as they grappled with their anxiety about the future, about life without the Master. Peter asked Jesus at the end of chapter 13, "Where are you going? Can we go, too?"

Our apprehensions reflect our era, as did theirs. What about social security? Will the money be there when I retire? Meanwhile, might I get cancer? Have a heart attack? Contract AIDS? One for a writer is to thank God for a new book in print, but will the next manuscript be published?

"Don't let your hearts be troubled," Jesus replied at the beginning of chapter 14. "Trust in God. Trust also in me."

Back in 1 Kings 17 is the story of the prophet Elijah who learned about trust in the crucible of danger. The land was ruled by an evil monarch, King Ahab, and his wife, Queen Jezebel. Those two did more, we're told, to provoke the wrath of God than all their predecessors combined. And Elijah, God's voice in that evil era, stood up to Ahab and Jezebel.

"As the Lord, the God of Israel, lives, whom I serve," he thundered, "there will be neither dew nor rain in the next few years except at my word" (v. 1).

No rain meant no crops and no water in the streams and wells. No water and no crops meant famine. Famine meant misery and discontent among Ahab's subjects. Even an absolute monarch is vulnerable when people grow desperate.

Being the instigating agent in this disaster reduced Elijah's popularity to a minus factor so low that God suggested he go on retreat to a remote little brook in the desert. Elijah hurried off with good cause for worry. Should Jezebel or Ahab lay hands on him, his life was over.

Let's leave him there for the moment. We will pick

up his story later and see what Elijah learned about stress management.

What Cures Worry?

Trust. Trust cures worry.

What's trust? Sounds too simple.

Trust? It is totally relying on the unlimited supply of the Trinity—God the Father, Jesus his Son, and the Holy Spirit. That's an acrostic: Totally relying on the unlimited supply of the Trinity. Trust.

Let's break it down. What does it mean to rely totally on God? As we take it apart and examine it, you'll see that trust is no passive, wimpy avoidance of reality. It involves choices that are neither easy for us nor natural to us. Trust is an absolute for Christian living, however, and learning how to trust develops spiritual muscle.

Begin with TR—*totally relying*. "Do not be anxious. Don't worry," Jesus said in Matthew 6:31. He elaborated at length in the following verses about the pitfalls of anxiety, but he didn't stop with the *don't*; in verse 33 he tells us what to do instead.

"Seek first [the Father's] kingdom and his righteousness, and all these things will be given to you as well."

We carry some responsibility when it comes to anxiety. These Scriptures suggest that we can exert some control over that to which we give our mental energies. We can choose not to be anxious, not to fret. Since your heavenly Father knows what you need, seek first his kingdom and righteousness and all else will be given to you as well.

How do you do that? What are the mechanics of

seeking his kingdom? Let me (Carroll) illustrate from what I learned in Korea.

In the early 1950s, the Korean peninsula was torn by war, a civil conflict in which several other nations participated in a power struggle between democracy and communism. Korean Christians suffered much at Communist hands and they, along with their nation, emerged at the ceasefire destitute and hungry, surrounded by rubble.

Rebuilding was top priority for South Korea. Homes, churches, places of business had been leveled in all but the southernmost tip of the peninsula. Stories circulated in those days of how Christians gathered to worship in the places where their churches once stood, maybe sheltered only by a piece of wall still standing or by charred beams that once supported gray roof tiles.

Even though their homes were as damaged as their churches, Korean Christians often set aside their anxieties about survival and chose to rebuild their churches before doing anything about their homes. Seek first the kingdom of God; antidote for worry, recipe for trust.

Totally relying also means rejoicing—always, Paul says in Philippians 4:4. Rejoice? Be happy, thankful, express joy over this mess? Rejoice that I'm facing bankruptcy? That my child is flunking out of school? That my marriage is cracking? That I'm alone?

It is neither easy nor natural to celebrate in the midst of disaster, but we can choose to do so, even though at first our choice is not backed up by any feeling of wanting to. We can choose to rejoice that God is present in whatever disaster threatens us, that we're not alone. We can also thank him that his limitless strength is available to us because Jesus redeemed us and we are his.

We both know a man, David, who learned this lesson at what had to be the most agonizing period of his life. His little daughter was dying of a cancerous brain tumor. In the midst of his pain God whispered a secret.

"Praise me. Find some reason to be thankful, something praiseworthy, even while your heart is breaking."

David learned his lesson and without fail still finds something praiseworthy in every difficulty he faces. He did *not* praise the Lord that his little girl died; he *did* find God worthy of praise even in moments of unspeakable pain.

Paul tells the Philippians and us that rather than struggling with anxiety, our time would be better spent in prayer and petition, presenting our requests to God with thanksgiving (4:6). He also says that God's peace will guard our hearts and minds.

It's like the businessman who prayed each day just before leaving his office. He tore off the calendar page for that day and stood holding it before God. "Lord," he said, "I know I've made mistakes today. I know too that I've succeeded at times. Whatever this day was or was not, I give it back to you."

He dropped the calendar page and all it represented into his wastebasket and headed home, trusting the Lord and guarded by his peace, choosing not to fall prey to second-guessing and anxiety.

The third ingredient in Paul's recipe for relying on God deals with what we think about. Again we make a choice. Fill our thinking, he tells us, with whatever is true, noble, right, pure, lovely, admirable, excellent, or praiseworthy (Phil. 4:8). That's a long list and if we commit ourselves to concentrating on it, to finding in every situation some of these qualities, worry will not dominate our minds. It can't. After all, we have only so much thinking time and if that time is filled with whatever is noble, pure, lovely, or praiseworthy, the injustices and what-ifs that threaten to haunt us cannot even hope for equal time inside our heads.

Totally relying also means spending, investing because you believe the returns will be worth the expenditure. We do it with our money, if we have any. People with lots of it play the stock market; people with less try to build up a little something in savings accounts because they believe the bankers will see to it that interest accrues and that their investment will grow.

But it won't happen unless they give over some dollars to banks and investment counselors. They must choose to trust, choose to spend in order to earn.

Let's get back to Elijah in the desert. Even *his* water source dries up finally and God has him on the move again. This part of his story illustrates the spending concept even though money doesn't figure in it at all. It deals with hunger versus satiety, life versus death, and, most pertinent to us, it tells us what God means by spending in order to learn how to trust.

Famine and drought have wrung Israel dry. Even Elijah, who predicted this disaster, is hungry so God tells him to go to Zarephath. "I have commanded a widow in that place to supply you with food," he says.

Elijah has been through plenty with God so he knows how to trust. He strides through the heat and dust to the gate of Zarephath where he sees a widow gathering sticks. As he sinks onto a stone in the shade of the town wall, he mops his face with his sleeve and calls out to the woman.

"Would you bring me a little water in a jar so I may have a drink?"

The woman nods courteously at the traveler and moves off toward the well.

"And bring me, please, a piece of bread."

The woman turns her worn, lined face toward the stranger resting in the shade. She knows from his clothes and wild mane that he is a prophet of God.

"As surely as the Lord your God lives, I don't have any bread—only a handful of flour in a jar and a little oil in a jug. I am gathering a few sticks to take home and make a meal for myself and my son, that we may eat it, and die."

Elijah hunches forward, one hand on his walking stick, and impales the woman with his blazing eyes. But his voice, rumbling from deep in his chest, is gentle.

"Don't be afraid. Go home and do as you have said. But first . . . make a small cake of bread for me from what you have and bring it to me, and then make something for yourself and your son."

The widow stares back into the prophet's eyes and her protests die within her. She weighs his preposterous demand.

"This is what the Lord, the God of Israel, says," he continues. " 'The jar of flour will not be used up and the jug of oil will not run dry until the day the Lord gives rain on the land.' "

The woman gazes at the prophet a moment longer as his words, God's words, war with her fear of starvation and death. Then, without speaking, she bends and bundles her sticks, hoists them to her head and walks slowly homeward (vv. 7–16).

The Bible says she did as Elijah told her. It also says, "There was food every day for Elijah and for the woman and her family." The flour was not used up and the jug of oil did not run dry. Because she agreed to spend something, she discovered the power available in totally relying on God.

After TR in the word 'trust' comes US. Totally relying on the *unlimited supply* of the Trinity. Unlimited?

Our Father, God, his Son, Jesus, and the comforting, enabling Holy Spirit command and control unlimited resources that are available to us because we choose to believe in Jesus as Savior. But how difficult it is for us to rely on their supply. Our way is to scurry about, trying to resolve our difficulties, to squirrel away our assets on the assumption that we must care for and solve everything that comes along. We don't have anything with which to compare God's method of supply in our human experience until we've walked with him for a while. Otherwise it's beyond our comprehension.

In John 14, the disciples' method of solving the dilemmas of life without Jesus was to insist that he stay with them. Life would be intolerable without his physical presence, they believed. But Jesus knew his way was better. If he left them, taking away his limiting physical presence, he could come back to them through the Holy Spirit and live within them. Not only that, he could activate God's plan that the entire world should learn of his love, something impossible unless he returned to the Father.

Before Elijah went to Zarephath and taught the widow about miraculous resources, he'd learned his own lesson out by the brook in the wilderness. The trickle of water cared for his thirst, and the Lord requisitioned a squadron of ravens to bring him food.

Talk about miracles! Ravens are birds of prey, quarrelsome carrion-pickers and eaters of insects. They don't care too well even for their own young. But when God chose them to nurture his weary, frightened, discouraged prophet, he mobilized this most unlikely species of bird to deliver . . . fresh meat . . . to Elijah!

Not only is the Lord's supply beyond comparison, it's also beyond comprehension. We cannot fathom all that he's done or all he can do. Our minds can't reach around all the resources and power he represents. Ephesians 3:8 calls this supply the "unsearchable riches of Christ." This is why the widow's flour and oil never ran out, limitless riches in our Father's hand.

God put these unsearchable, unknowable riches into figures we can use to approach understanding by utilizing a psalm-writer's talent. Psalm 50:10–12 says, "Every animal of the forest is mine, and the cattle on a thousand hills. I know every bird in the mountains, and the creatures of the field are mine. If I were hungry I would not tell you, for the world is mine, and all that is in it."

A father watched his small son try to move a big rock. The boy pushed and heaved, huffed and sighed. Finally he flopped down on the grass and leaned against his project, wiping sweat off his face with a grimy hand.

His dad walked over and hunkered down by his winded little boy. "Have you tried everything you can to move this?" he asked.

"Well, sure, Dad. Didn't you see me? I used all my muscles to try and make it move."

"I disagree," said his father. "You haven't done everything you can."

"I don't see what else I could've done."

"You could have asked me."

The little boy had ignored the major resource available to him in the person of his father who stood by, itching to put his much more significant strength into moving the rock for his son. But the boy forgot to ask.

Don't we ignore God at times, even though he is our bottomless resource? His limitless supply is beyond our comprehension, yet we huff and heave at our pet projects or problems, never asking him to apply his power to the situation. All we need to do is to ask him and trust him.

A missionary once told Charles, my (Vicki's) husband, that in Japanese the ideogram, or word picture, for trust is an earthenware jar with the bottom knocked out. No, it isn't broken and useless; it is a conduit for supply not limited by the "facts" of maximum volume statistics or knowable capacity. That's God's supply to us when we trust him.

The last part of our trust acrostic is T for Trinity. Look at John 14 again. In verse 20 Jesus tells his followers, "On that day [when they can no longer see him in the world but when he dwells in them through the Holy Spirit] you will realize that I am in my Father, and you are in me, and I am in you."

By the way, have you noticed that for every absolute we're studying that came from Jesus himself in John 13–15, he says either, "I will, I have," or "I am"? Strong, simple, clear. All that is required of us is reliance on his assertions.

So as Jesus prepared the disciples, and us, for what life will be like without his physical presence, he says, "Don't let your heart be troubled . . . I am in you." And the Holy Spirit, member of the Trinity whose job it is to comfort and communicate with our spirits, dwells within us, if invited.

In 2 Timothy 1:12, Paul wrote, "I am not ashamed, because I know whom I have believed, and am convinced that he is able to guard what I have entrusted to him for that day." Paul was convinced, persuaded, that God would protect and care for that with which he trusted him, whatever it was. Past regrets, future worries, needs, joys, hopes can all be placed in his hands for safekeeping because he alone merits our trust.

Society disagrees, however. Today's idea is to trust in ourselves because we are to be our own lifeguard. But the Bible offers a different idea. In its pages we're told that we *can* trust in God who lives in us through the Holy Spirit, that we *cannot* depend on ourselves.

Why not? Because every time we try it, we mess up. Proverbs 28:26 says, "He who trusts in himself is a fool." This is not talking about self-confidence. We all need some of that. But to trust in ourselves for life's answers, ignoring God, is a fool's venture.

The same is true for trusting in people. Again,

we're not talking about being trusting and loving. But to depend on human beings exclusively without guidance from the divine inner voice is to end up confused and misled. Only God can supply what we need. "It is better to take refuge in the Lord than to trust in man" (Ps. 118:8).

The same goes for riches and material possessions. Money to buy whatever we want gives a sense of security, as do elaborate protection systems. It is easy to be lulled into trust in the power of unlimited resources, but look at another ageless proverb. "Whoever trusts in his riches will fall, but the righteous will thrive like a green leaf" (Prov. 11:28).

"Some trust in chariots and some in horses [gilt-edged investments and armed security guards?], but we trust in the name of the Lord our God. They are brought to their knees and fall, but we rise up and stand firm" (Ps. 20:7–8).

E. Stanley Jones, missionary, author, and speaker, in *The Divine Yes* writes after suffering a paralyzing stroke,

> They say that in Switzerland the Swiss climbers have a rope the strands of which in the center are the strongest and are capable of holding up a man if all the edges of the rope have worn off. The inmost strands are the strongest. I have found that to be true of Christian experience. Many of the strands of my life have been broken by this stroke for I can no longer preach and I cannot write as my eyesight is so poor that I cannot see my own writing. I can only dictate in a tape recorder. The things that were dear to me for the time being are broken. The innermost strands belonging to the Kingdom and the person of Jesus and my experience of him hold me as much as the total rope for the innermost strands are the

strongest. I need no outer props to hold up my faith for my faith holds me. So I do not possess my faith, it possesses me.[1]

Trust: A simple, single-syllable word, but complex, powerful, and life-changing in the living out of its meaning.

The two men finally came through the Tokyo crowds to where I (Carroll) waited in the gathering dusk. I had no alternative but to trust that they'd eventually come. That's not the whole story, though. The Comforter had stood there with me as Protector, Consoler, and Friend. He's the trustworthy one and it was he who saw all of us safely home at last.

*   *   *

Lord, could you pry my fingers loose from the controls? Teach me how to trust. My culture doesn't understand this and so my point of view is to depend on my skills and resources. But I'd like to relax a little and totally rely (my part) on the unlimited resources of the Trinity (your part). Let's begin today with the little stuff. I trust you to make it a way of life for me.

What Do You Think?

1. What does trusting God mean to you?

2. Are you going through a difficult situation now? What is it, and how are you trusting or not trusting God?

3. What does Matthew 6:25 mean when it says, "Do not worry"?

4. In 1 Kings 17, how did Elijah have to trust?

5. What was first required of the widow before the supply of oil and the meal would be unending? How does this relate to our trusting the Lord?

Note

[1] E. Stanley Jones, *The Divine Yes* (Nashville: Abingdon, 1975), 63.

4

obey

Read John 14:15–27 and
2 Kings 5:1–27

PHILIP PLAYED under the huge tree, untroubled by Africa's midday heat. This was home to him and his missionary family, as natural a habitat as an Ohio farm is to another. Suddenly his father called out sharply from across the yard.

"Philip! Obey me instantly. Get down on your stomach."

Philip flopped down on his belly, eyes fastened on his dad.

"Now crawl toward me—fast!"

The child wormed part way across the space that divided him from his tense father who spoke again, "Stand up now, and run to me."

Philip stood safe within the circle of his father's arms. As he looked back, he saw hanging from the tree branch under which he'd been playing a fifteen-foot snake.[1]

Obedience. No whys, no whines of "yes, but . . ."

For Philip obedience was a life-and-death matter; for us, maybe not—and maybe so. We can't know, often, what the results will be, but we can know that obedience is an absolute for Christian living, one that goes hand in hand with trust. The little boy under the tree trusted his father, so when dad spoke, he responded without question . . . at least that time.

The father could see the danger that hung literally over his son's head. His point of view required instant and absolute obedience without questions or explanations. The father spoke, and the child obeyed. What if Philip had not done as his father so abruptly commanded? Not a pleasant thought. The lesson for us is obvious, isn't it? Our heavenly Father can see the total picture as it relates to our lives, but we cannot, which is why obedience is crucial in Christian living.

Obedience is hard. What Christian has not asked, "How can I know God's will for me, his total life-long plan?" Pondering those years of obeying and following that stretch out from today to eternity can grow into more than we can face. It's as if I (Vicki) said to my younger daughter, "All right, honey, here's a list of all the things I want you to do this month. You listen and I'll read them to you. I expect you to obey each item on the list."

We know better than to do this and so does God, which is why he parcels out his plan to us, piece by piece. Our responsibility is to act on what we know, obeying what we know to obey. As we do he reveals more, little by little. Probably Philip's father knew through his child's previous behavior patterns that he could expect the boy to respond to his brusque, unexplained order because he was an obedient child. He trusted his dad and wanted to please him.

What does obedience mean? To carry out the order of, or to be guided by, is what the dictionary says. My (Vicki's) little girl defines it as "doing what I am told instead of not doing what I am told." Not bad. Simple, easy to understand, and applicable to all ages. The Bible is absolutely clear on the matter of obedience. It's there cover to cover, a recurring theme. Right from the beginning in the Garden of Eden the first man and woman failed to obey God and their disobedience affects us yet. Read Genesis 2 and 3. From there on through to the end, the Bible stresses "Obey, obey."

Jesus said, "If you love me, obey me" (John 14:15, Living Bible). Other versions word it "obey what I command" (NIV) or "keep my commandments" (KJV). But however the translators word it, his meaning is clear and absolute.

So if we believe Jesus is God's son and have entrusted our lives into his care, why would we ever disobey him?

Causes of Disobedience

Lack of love. "If you love me you will obey me." Any parent or teacher knows an obedient child is a loving child and God feels the same way. He knows when we obey him that it is because we love him. Obedience proves our love. John 14:15, 21, and 23 point out that love motivates obedience between the Lord and us. Note how he stresses this by repetition; then verse 24 reverses it for emphasis. "Anyone who doesn't obey me doesn't love me."

Imagine yourself in Philip's shoes. Some outsized authority figure interrupts your fun by barking out an unexplained order. Authority figures turn you off anyway so you glare across the yard and accuse him of spoiling your fun. Hardly a loving response to someone you care for.

Perhaps lack of love ties in with an over-inflated view of ourselves, such as *pride* can create. In a remarkable story of servants and kings, we see in the Old Testament how pride can threaten obedience even in life-and-death situations.

Naaman was commander in chief for the king of Aram, with all the power and privilege that position entailed. But disaster threatened all that Naaman held within his grasp because he was a leper. He stared into an abyss of loathsome disease, social ostracism, and, of course, death.

In Naaman's household worked a slave girl from Israel who knew God, so she boldly suggested that he seek out "the prophet who is in Samaria." He would cure him of his leprosy, she promised.

After a couple of detours, Naaman pulled up in front of Elisha's door in a cloud of dust stirred up by the retinue traveling with him. Elisha sent word to the general by messenger: "Go wash yourself seven times in the Jordan, and your flesh will be restored and you will be cleansed."

Naaman was outraged by the whole ridiculous scenario. Here he stood like a petitioner at the door of some religious fanatic in the provinces only to be told by a lackey to dunk himself in the Jordan River when he had rivers aplenty in Damascus.

In a rage Naaman wheeled his chariot about and left, his staff clattering after him. Incensed by the prophet's failure to acknowledge his rank, Naaman's pride kept him stiffly aboard his chariot—and still a dying leper—rather than immersed in an insignificant stream, humbled and whole.

As you read the rest of the story (2 Kings 5:1–27), you learn that Naaman, at the urging of servants, managed at last in his desperation to bring himself to obey the prophet and was healed when he bathed in the Jordan.

But a footnote to his story gives us our third and fourth causes of disobedience, *greed* and *lack of fear*. After Naaman's healing he became as generous as he'd been haughty just a short time before. Dismounting this time before Elisha's house, he stood before the man of God.

"Now I know that there is no God in all the world except in Israel," Naaman said. "Please accept now a gift from your servant."

"As surely as the Lord lives, whom I serve, I will not accept a thing." The prophet refused Naaman's offer of lavish rewards. But listening to their conversation was Elisha's servant, Gehazi. His interest stirred at the thought of riches offered by the grateful general.

Naaman and company left for home and Gehazi pelted after him. Again Naaman, washed clean of pride as well as leprosy, stepped down from his chariot to meet the panting runner.

"Is everything all right?" he asked.

Gehazi made up a hoax to con Naaman out of a couple of bags of money for "some traveling young prophets."

"By all means," boomed the happy general, and

along with money he pressed a couple of sets of clothing into Gehazi's willing, greedy hands.

Back at Elisha's house Gehazi squirreled away his loot and reported in to Elisha.

"Where've you been?" the prophet asked.

"Nowhere," Gehazi answered.

But Elisha knew better and told Gehazi so. "Is this the time to take money, or to accept clothes?" he thundered at the greedy culprit. "Naaman's leprosy will cling to you and to your descendants forever."

Gehazi lived with the prophet Elisha and had heard him refuse rewards for Naaman's miraculous return to health. He could not plead ignorance of what was right and wrong. He worked for a man whom God had chosen as his voice, his word for that era.

Obviously, Gehazi did not fear the consequences of disobedience. Having served Elisha, he must have witnessed the results of sin but hardened himself against them. *Lack of fear* can so easily free people to sin when they are determined to follow the path of disobedience.

But *ignorance of God's Word* certainly can contribute to disobedience. The Lord, mindful of this, directed one of the earliest leaders of Israel about this possibility. "Do not let this Book of the Law depart from your mouth," he ordered Joshua. "Meditate on it day and night, so that you may be careful to do everything written in it. Then you will be prosperous and successful" (Josh. 1:8).

The Book of the Law that Joshua was to meditate on twenty-four hours a day contained much less information about God and his plans for us than

does our Bible. We can know the major part of God's
will for us by searching his book, the Bible.

I (Carroll) can remember early in my Sunday
school days memorizing Psalm 119:11. In the NIV it
reads, "I have hidden your word in my heart that I
might not sin against you." Of course I learned it in
the King James Version since that was many years
ago. But whatever the translation, the whole psalm is
crammed with references to the guidance of the
Word of God and how ignorance of his Word leaves
the path we've followed pock-marked with the
pitfalls of our disobedience.

In Hebrews 3, the writer includes a section that
warns his readers, and us, against *unbelief.* He cites
the disasters suffered by the Israelis who wandered
in the desert, ever failing to learn the basic lesson
that God expected them to obey him. Verses 16–18
raise a series of rhetorical questions, one of which
asks, "To whom did God swear that they would
never enter his rest if not to those who disobeyed? So
we see that they were not able to enter, because of
their unbelief."

A friend once told a woman who was known for
her strong commitment to obey God, "I think that if
God spoke from the clouds and said, 'Jump through
that stone wall,' you'd do it. If you were sure he
wanted you to, would you try it?"

"I would," the woman replied, "and I'd expect
God to make a hole."

That's belief. And here's where trust and obedience go hand in hand. You can trust someone with
your life only when you know that person cares
about you and has your best interests in mind when
he asks something of you. That should be our

attitude toward God. We should trust him so much that we obey his every directive. Trust and belief, earlier absolutes we've already studied, are building blocks for our obedience.

The Old Testament shows us on page after page how God strove to teach his beloved people the importance of obedience. The major obstacle, which time and again they failed to clear, was their own *stubbornness*. The prophet Jeremiah contended with this problem as the Jewish kingdoms crumbled under attack from their neighbors. He spoke out against their sin and failure to follow God in the seventh chapter of his Old Testament book.

God speaks: "I gave them this command: Obey me, and I will be your God and you will be my people. Walk in all the ways I command you, that it may go well with you. But they did not listen or pay attention; instead, they followed the stubborn inclinations of their evil hearts. They went backward and not forward" (vv. 23–24).

One stubborn child in a classroom creates misery for the whole group. One stubborn committee member causes stalemate and thwarts progress. The whole business of this book is discovery of God's absolutes, the non-negotiables of walking with him. His commands are just that, imperatives that end with a period. But like the people of the Old Testament (and people ever since, for that matter) we keep trying to change that period into a question mark with our "whys," and the clear imperative into a host of exceptions: "yes, but . . ." and "but I want. . . ."

I (Vicki) recall when I tried to change one of God's periods into a question mark. My husband and I had been asked to consider a year of ministry in Australia. After four long, hard years of working to put myself through college because I felt God wanted me to teach, I had taught only one year. I couldn't understand why I should give it up nor did I want to consider a change. In my heart I knew it was right, but I was too stubborn to submit.

Only after a serious car accident and as I lay in the hospital reading *There I Stood in All My Splendor* by Ethel Barrett did I submit to God's call. These words gripped me: "From time to time our course may change; if we are wholly His it is not a mistake but another stepping stone in the complete plan."[2]

By the way, our year in Australia was one of the most challenging and fruitful years of our lives.

Certain things are not negotiable if we've committed our lives into the hands of our Creator. He expects implicit obedience, willingness to jump through stone walls, if you will. He also expects us to trust his choices for us whether they be the clearly stated laws and behavior requirements he's given us in the Bible or the personalized guidance he whispers to us alone as we learn to hear his gentle voice.

Consequences of Obedience

Consequences crop up in the Bible whichever path we choose, consequences of disobedience and those of obedience. Let's focus on the outcome of our obedience to God. Go back again to John 14 where the results of obedience are spelled out.

First is love, two-way love. "Whoever has my commands and obeys them, he is the one who loves me" (v. 21a). Knowing and obeying God's plan shows him and the world that we love him. Then it says, "He who loves me [evidenced by our obedience] will be loved by my Father, and I too will love him and show myself to him" (v. 21b).

Must we obey God then before he will love us? Is it so conditional as this? No, that's not what it means. God's love for us is unfailing. It is always there, no matter how we wobble or stray.

Maybe it is similar to one of those lovely days when my (Vicki's) girls are obedient and tractable, responsive to my guidance without veering off on paths of their own choosing. I love them no matter how naughty their actions. But when they respond and obey me, my heart runs over with loving appreciation for them and for the warm rapport between us. I can sense their love for me specially well at times like that and it fills me with joy.

A progression occurs as we set out on the path of obedience. As we obey the Lord and discover new depths of his love for us and ours for him, the more we'll discover about Christ as he shows himself more and more clearly to us. Verse 23 adds Jesus' promise that he and the Father will make their home with those who obey him. What an incredible idea! God at home within me.

So we decide to obey God even though we don't know all that obedience will mean. As a result, we experience new dimensions of our love-fueled relationship with him. And then we learn more about our Lord as he entrusts us with more knowledge and understanding. Peace floods our minds and hearts because of the way we have chosen. "Peace I leave with you" (v. 27).

Don't misunderstand. Having his peace doesn't

mean a trouble-free, smooth-sailing life. Stories in
the Bible of people in crisis like David, Daniel, Ruth,
Paul, and Job set us straight on that score. But it does
mean that in the teeth of the storm we can know
interior serenity because we know whose we are and
we know ourselves to be faithful, obedient followers
of our Lord.

The Bible is full of information about obedience, a
fact that makes us know how important this is to
God and therefore how crucial to us, his followers.
Look up this list of Bible references. Take time to
write down what each one has to say about the
consequences of obedience.

Exodus 19:5; 23:21–22
Deuteronomy 5:29; 11:26–27; 28:1–14
Isaiah 1:19–20
James 1:25

Cures for Disobedience

Unlike Philip who responded without a whimper
or hesitation to his father's command to come away
from the danger the snake posed (though the boy
didn't even know about it), we don't always respond
readily to God's direction. We don't want to because
we have other ideas of what we'd like to do. We
don't want to leave our toys and the shade of the tree
just because our Father says we must.

How does God help us deal with this? Intellectual-
ly we know obedience is necessary, and spiritually
we'd like to be better followers. So what can we do?

Turn again to John 14. In the middle of Christ's
commands to obey he tells us that the Holy Spirit

will teach us all things and will remind us of everything he has said (v. 26).

A young man, hungry to understand more about the Holy Spirit, went on a private retreat. A friend, knowing of his search, quizzed him upon his return.

"Good retreat?"

"Well, yes and no," replied the seeker.

"Didn't you learn anything about the Holy Spirit?"

"Yes, but not so much as I'd hoped."

"Tell me this, then," his questioner continued, "did you learn anything about Jesus Christ?"

"Oh, yes. I learned much more about Jesus—who he is and what he is and what he does in my life—than I've ever known before. Jesus has become so real to me!"

"Well, then," his friend observed, "the Holy Spirit did his job. That's who he is, the One who tells us who Jesus is."

The Holy Spirit's role in our quest to learn to obey God is to remind us to do it. For years I (Carroll) had trouble disciplining myself to keep a daily devotional time with the Lord. For hours on end I could read for pleasure with no trouble at all. I even managed to get to the office on time and do a decent amount of housework without outside nagging. But I found it so easy to forget that a whole day had gone by without any time spent with my heavenly Father.

I begged the Lord to help me. I knew he wanted me to meet him daily and I wanted to, but my ability to obey was underdeveloped, to say the least. In response to my asking, our faithful Counselor, the Holy Spirit, now whispers in my ear to remind me that my day is slipping away and I haven't yet talked with God. He'll pursue me when I'm in the middle of a page of writing. (I shall have to leave this as soon as I finish telling you my story.) Or he'll remind me at the end of a hectic day that I can't sleep yet. Finally my slow, lazy, stubborn heart has learned to take time for conversation with the Lord. And I've learned to be thankful for the Holy Spirit even when I've wished that he'd leave me alone.

Not only does the Holy Spirit, in curing our disobedience, teach and remind us, he helps us love. Romans 5:5 says, "God has poured out his love into our hearts by the Holy Spirit." Back to the love business again, which must mean that love is the major factor in obeying.

Perhaps the best way we can learn how to make obedience to God a part of our lives is to observe someone else's example. Try Jesus. In Hebrews we learn that he petitioned with loud cries and tears the one who could save him from death, but even though he was God's Son "he learned obedience" (5:7–9). Because of his obedience we receive through him our eternal salvation.

Often obedience is not easy. It was not easy for Jesus, the Bible tells us. But because he submitted to God's plan, accepting his Father's will over his own, we can be redeemed. God may not ask us to perform some lofty, sacrificial task. Maybe all he wants is for us to obey his rules for daily living or to respond when the Holy Spirit nudges us to take some action.

He nudged me (Vicki) late one Saturday night when I was tired and yearning to stretch out between the sheets and sleep. But I kept thinking of a friend at church, a perky gal whose feathers, I'd noticed, were drooping. So I sighed, postponed sleep, and went to my study to write and tell her of my love and regard for her.

Next morning I tucked the note into my friend's mailbox at church. She stopped me after the evening service and said, "You don't know what your note meant to me. Last week I felt as if I didn't have a friend in the world. Yet when I read what you wrote, I knew I did."

As I walked out of the church I thanked the Lord for giving me the help and strength I needed to obey him, to do what he wanted me to do.

*   *   *

Lord Jesus, I believe you are who the Bible says you are. I love you because you loved me first. Now teach me, please, to obey you, to keep your laws that I read in Scripture, and to respond when the Holy Spirit whispers your directives to me. And when I think my way might be better than yours, help me to trust you and then to follow your path instead of mine.

What Do You Think?

Read John 14:15–27

1. What blessings come to those who obey God?

2. Who helps us obey? (Also read Phil. 2:13.)

Read 1 Samuel 15:18–23

3. What did King Saul's disobedience cost him?

Read 2 Kings 5:1–27

4. What lessons can we learn from Naaman's Jewish servant girl?

5. What finally prompted Naaman's obedience?

Read Acts 5:29

6. When does obeying God rather than people become difficult?

Notes

[1] Paraphrased from Donald Grey Barnhouse, *Let Me Illustrate* (Westwood, N.J.: Revell, 1967), 231.

[2] Ethel Barrett, *There I Stood in All My Splendor* (Glendale, Calif.: Regal, 1966), 184.

5
love

Read John 15:9–26

STEVE PACED his office, frowning at the carpet. It was time to go home but he didn't want to. Why should he? Exchanging the ego-building attentions of a competent, courteous staff for the intermittent nit-picking of a perfectionist wife did not pull him toward the commuter traffic choking the streets outside.

Several of his friends, for one reason or another, had fallen into the easy liaisons that develop between co-workers, pursuing a fantasy sort of love. Steve understood how this can happen and had been tempted himself.

But Steve was a Christian. He'd been searching through the pages of his Bible to discover what God has to say about love. He'd found some tough stuff there. Love is of God, he read. It was not created to satisfy his ego but to teach him about his Creator. Examples from Scripture taught him that love is tough, hard work, sometimes a commitment not based on emotion.

So Steve decided to love his wife with God's help, not because he felt floods of romantic emotion, not because she always made him feel good, but because the act of loving is a command from God and because he promised to do so on their wedding day, a vow he couldn't find reasons to rescind as he studied his Bible. So he shrugged into his topcoat, picked up his briefcase, and headed toward his car. As he did, his spirits lifted just a bit. Odd, he thought, to find a deep well of satisfaction and something akin to the warmth of joy down inside as he did something he really didn't want to do.

Steve's story is not a scenario for the excitement of love as our culture defines it in movies, best-selling novels, or television. Nor does it resemble the self-gratifying drives found in the lyrics of pop music. If we pay too much attention to the hype that surrounds us, we may begin to believe that love is the private domain of the young, the rich, or the overheated.

But the Bible tells a different story. Biblical love is not a feeling one falls into; it is an action one chooses to take. To love is a verb, an action word. Read our Scripture selection listed at the beginning of this chapter.

Here and elsewhere in the Bible we see that we're expected, commanded, to love as Jesus loves—an absolute. His example of how this is done is there for us to read and imitate. Steve began to learn this as he grappled with his negative feelings about his wife and chose to deal with them in a Christ-like manner. He also learned that after he chose to act on one of

God's commandments, power to do what he didn't feel like doing began to aid and energize him. Even fickle feelings begin to cooperate.

"Boy! I don't know," you're saying, "doesn't sound like love to me. Sounds like work. Who can love like that?"

Nobody says it's easy. Remember Jesus in the garden. He agonized over the lengths his love was taking him. Let's look at what's involved and see what we can learn.

Requirement to Love

"My command is this: Love each other as I have loved you" (John 15:12). Jesus repeated this imperative and in almost identical words in verse 17. A new commandment, he called it back in chapter 13, but it was the same idea: Love one another as Jesus loves us. "All men will know that you are my disciples, if you love one another" (v. 35).

Jesus said it just before his crucifixion to his disciples, that group of some of the most mismatched individuals anyone ever tried to mold into a sales force. How could jealous competitors for places of honor, men who'd known only the narrow confines of village life, blustery cowards, and minor government officials with wobbly ethics ever meet the basic requirement of loving one another? Even so, Jesus met the challenge head on.

"All men will know that you are my disciples, if you love one another." Jesus' goal for his selfish crew was that they demonstrate the kind of love that turns the world upside down, thereby introducing it to its Savior.

"Move beyond your selfishness, your greed, your jealousy, your inability to forgive . . . and learn to love each other. Only then can you tell the world about me with authority." That's what Jesus was telling the disciples and all of us who have ever sought to follow. "Love each other as I love you."

Responsibility of Love

Love sacrifices unconditionally. The supreme example of unconditional love is Jesus' death on the cross coupled with God's plan to send him there to build a bridge between himself and his beloved world.

Does this mean we should seek death on behalf of someone we love in order to prove we love unconditionally? No, not as a goal. Individuals have died as substitutes for loved ones; history and literature are full of such stories, but loving unconditionally is not limited to dying. There's more to this than physical sacrifice. Living for them is better.

What sacrifices, then, do we find in loving?

The first could be time, that precious commodity in our fast-paced world. Loving friends make time for each other. Dads and moms give up the newspaper's sports page or twenty minutes in a bubble bath to go over spelling words or help with math problems. Or a young mother surrenders the significant material advantages she could earn by pursuing her career, trading them for emotionally healthy children secure in her presence at home.

Then, what about the sacrifice of our material resources, money or goods, for the love of someone even when it means a personal squeeze? Love gives even when it hurts.

Love shares unconditionally. In John 15:14 Jesus says, "You are my friends if you do what I command." Then he goes on to explain why he calls them friends instead of servants. "I have called you friends, for everything that I learned from my Father I have made known to you" (v. 15).

Jesus shared from his heart all that the Father told him. If you take some extra time and flip through all four gospels, you will see how Jesus spent important blocks of time teaching the twelve about God's purposes for his Son's time on earth, his plan to redeem the world, and his incredible love that fueled it all.

Jesus laid it all out for them, risking and experiencing their confusion and incredulity in the face of such a plan. He even endured their rejection and denial, but because he loved them so much, he stood transparent and vulnerable before them, a perfect example of loving and sharing without reservation.

Love selects unconditionally. "You did not choose me," Jesus said to the twelve, "but I chose you" (15:16). The disciples needed reassurance that Jesus selected them as recipients of his love. Even though he saw their faults and foibles, he also recognized their potential and their strengths.

Don't misunderstand. This doesn't mean that Jesus loved only his disciples and shunned the remainder of the human race. As you read about his life and ministry, you can see that that isn't true. He's teaching them and us that to love as he loves means to do it unconditionally, to love everyone, to choose to do so even when they don't love us back.

Some people are impossible to love, aren't they? We naturally love those who love us while we respond with hostility and resentment to rude drivers on the road, or with fear and dislike to anyone who menaces our well-being.

Jesus told his friends that he chose to love them in spite of their flaws and inadequacies. So it follows that he expects us to branch out and choose to love beyond our safe, familiar spheres.

Results of Love

Joy. In John 15:10, Jesus speaks of obedience and how it expresses love. Then in the next sentence (v. 11) he explains why he talked about such things. "I have told you this so that my joy may be in you and that your joy may be complete."

Our businessman friend at the beginning of this chapter was discovering this. As he made the tough yet godly choice to love even when he didn't feel like it, he began to experience stirrings of joy in the deep places of his soul.

Joy and happiness are not the same. Joy can abide even within unhappy situations while happiness depends on circumstances. Joy depends on God's presence within us and the peace he brings to our lives. So if we love one another, it produces joy.

Fruit. "I chose you to go and bear fruit—fruit that will last" (v. 16). In the last chapter we learned that if we love God we will obey him. Here we see that to love means to bear fruit. In another place the Bible says we're known by the fruit we produce.

Fruit-bearing is a commonly used biblical term, but what does it really mean? To bear fruit means what it sounds like; to produce apples if you're an apple tree, apricots if you're an apricot tree. But the idea is to produce. If you are a believer in and a follower of the Lord Jesus Christ, then you live like one and act like one. You obey his directions, especially in loving one another. That's bearing fruit.

Hostility. This, sadly enough, can result from our love for our Lord and for one another. Jesus talked about this. "If the world hates you, keep in mind that it hated me first. If you belonged to the world, it would love you as its own. As it is, you do not belong to the world, but I have chosen you out of the world. That is why the world hates you" (vv. 18–19).

He goes on to talk about his being persecuted by the world he created, and he tells us that "no servant is greater than his master." This means that we can expect difficulties because of our identification with Jesus just as he experienced hostility when he was here.

"The world" is another term used often in the Bible and in that context it means "human society organizing itself against God." No doubt you can sense the existence of elements around you that are organized against God. This is hard at times for believers to admit—it seems so old-fashioned and strait-laced—but the aware Christian knows they are there.

Sometimes, for love of our Savior and in obedience to what we know about how he expects his followers to behave, we must risk hostility from those around us, from the world, by saying no when they want us to say yes. Or by speaking up when they want us to keep still.

We must not condemn or criticize those who don't love the Master and who have not yet chosen to follow him as we have. Part of bearing fruit is to maintain a loving attitude even in the face of someone else's disgruntlement with our behavior. Remember how Jesus acted during his betrayal, trial, and crucifixion?

In John 15:21 Jesus explains why hostility is part of the results of love. "They will treat you this way," he said, "because of my name, for they do not know the One who sent me." Down through history from earliest times people's ignorance about God and his love have promoted grim atrocities against believers. They didn't know him. But you do! You know God the Father, who sent Jesus to us, because you chose to believe on him and to follow him.

Worse than ignorance, perhaps, is the fact that hostility against Christ's love results from plain old sin. Because Jesus came and taught us so clearly about sin, about right and wrong, those who've been confronted by his teaching and chosen to ignore it are guilty of sin (v. 22).

Christian behavior, and by this we mean moral uprightness, honesty, loving those around us, obeying God's laws, and sharing our faith causes guilt feelings for those who do not live this way (vv. 23–24).

Relief From the World's Hatred

How do we deal with hostility, the animosity that Christian love can generate?

First of all, as we've noticed before, we're promised the Counselor, the Comforter, and he is here not just to make us feel better but to give us wisdom and guidance in dealing with conflicts, hassles, and confrontations. John 15:26–27 talks about the role of the Holy Spirit, who is our Counselor. He'll speak through us about the Lord. "He will testify about me," it says, "but *you also must testify*" (our emphasis). We can't put our mouths and our actions in neutral and do nothing.

I (Vicki) faced this at our school's Parent-Teacher Organization board meeting. We needed to raise money and talk of a raffle came up. I have strong feelings about gambling, and I began to squirm as I thought about children of six, seven, and eight years selling raffle tickets and learning thereby that gambling is a good thing. I thought about the destructive, wasteful compulsion that some people struggle with all their lives and I couldn't sit silent knowing we could be unleashing this problem for even one of tomorrow's adults.

Of course the other side of the argument came back at me. What will these people think if I speak against such an ordinary, time-worn method of raising funds? They'll sneer at the poor little narrow-minded pastor's wife and write me off as just another religious nut. And what if they ask me, "If no raffle, what do you suggest? Any better ideas?"

My Counselor, the Holy Spirit, came through right on time. Even as he nudged me to "testify" to what I believed was God's will in this situation, he was also my Comforter because he protected me from excessive hostility. And because I said what I was supposed to, the board shifted to talk of an auction instead of the raffle. And everything worked out just fine.

My prayer was that if I opened my big mouth, the Holy Spirit would do the talking because I might mess it up. And he did even though, because I was a minority voice, I feared to say what I felt so strongly. But Jesus says we don't have to do these things alone; the Holy Spirit who lives in us does it through us.

In Romans 5:5 are words that can minister to us when someone hurts or misunderstands us. It says that God pours his love through us, again by the good graces of the Comforter. So all we have to do is keep the channel clear and he does the loving through us.

That was Steve's answer, the profound solution he was learning. He didn't know how to love his difficult wife, didn't even want to. But he chose to open his heart as a channel and let God do the loving where he could not.

Luke 6:27–35 gives tough, clear lessons on love in the face of hostility. Love your enemies. Do good to those who hate you. Bless those who curse you. Pray for those who mistreat you. Do to others as you would have them do to you. The last is an old friend; mother always trotted this one out when my brother and I (Carroll) were fighting.

This may be one of the most difficult sections in the Bible for us to absorb and obey. What impossible, unnatural behavior! Who does such things?

Yet there it is, absolutely clear as can be. No room for interpretation or argument. It goes on to ask, "What credit is that to you?" if we merely love those who love us. Jesus wants us to love our *enemies*. It finishes by telling us that herein lies great reward.

A consummate expression of God-given love appears in 1 Samuel 24. Saul was king, but David had been appointed his successor. Saul grappled with towering jealousy and anger that a shepherd boy should be so handsome, so strong, so gifted, so honored by the whole nation. So Saul set out to destroy the young man who had been like a son to him.

On Saul's way home from battling the Philistines, he heard that David and his men were hiding in the desert, so he took 3,000 Israelite troops to hunt David down. During the hunt Saul passed a cave and took the opportunity to step inside and relieve himself, unaware that David and his men crouched in the dark at the back. David's troops could not believe their eyes as they peered at the unmistakable silhouette of King Saul outlined against the mouth of the cave.

"This is it!" one hissed in David's ear. "This is the very day the Lord spoke of when he said to you, 'I will give your enemy into your hands for you to deal with as you wish.'"

David crept along the clammy wall, knife glinting in his hand. He paused by the robe King Saul had dropped on his way in. Seizing a corner of the garment, he sliced away a section of cloth and stuffed it into his belt. Then he stole back to his men, ignoring their disgust.

As Saul finished what he'd come into the cave to do, he turned and scooped up his robe as he strode back into the sunlight. David stood slowly and watched him go. He felt he'd done wrong.

"The Lord forbid," he said to his men, "that I should do such a thing to my master, the Lord's anointed, or lift my hand against him; for he is the anointed of the Lord."

David forbade his open-mouthed, disgruntled soldiers to attack Saul. As Saul and his 3,000 prepared to move on, David stepped out of the cave alone and called out to Saul.

"My lord the king!"

Saul whirled at the sound of that beloved, hated voice. Then David bowed to his king.

"Why do you listen," he asked, "when men tell you that I am bent on harming you? See how the Lord put you within my reach but I could not lift my hand against you. You are the Lord's anointed. Look at this!"

David held up before the king the scrap of cloth he'd cut from Saul's clothes. "Now understand and recognize . . . I have not wronged you . . . but you are hunting my life. May the Lord be our judge and decide between us."

Saul stared at the man in the mouth of the cave. Then he dropped his head and sobbed aloud before the thousands of soldiers who stood frozen in place by the spectacle of Israel's king undone by David's love and respect for him in spite of his own duplicity.

David could not peer ahead into the future and know how his willingness to love in obedience to God's direction would be rewarded. But he did it anyway.

Steve could not be sure that the early satisfaction he discovered in doing what was right in God's eyes would blossom into a love-filled, happy marriage, but he could know he was obeying God's plan for him.

All any of us can be sure of when we embark on a commitment to follow Jesus' example and love one another is that we're obeying him and following the path he set for us. And it's becoming clear, isn't it, that the longer we walk this Christian path the more joy outweighs the pain?

*   *   *

Okay, Lord, this week I will try to love someone who is a source of difficulty or problem. You know this is not natural or easy for me, so stand close by, will you, and keep reminding me how to do this?

What Do You Think?

1. What was Jesus' reason for telling his disciples about love? John 15:11

2. What is God's commandment concerning love? John 13:34; 15:12; 17:26; 2 John 5

3. What happens when we love? 1 John 4:12–18

4. What does God do for his enemies? Romans 5:10

5. How did David respond to King Saul? 1 Samuel 24–25. What would you have done?

6

serve

Read John 13:1–17

IN HIS SHORT life Trevor had never heard of anything so terrible. As he and his parents watched the evening news in their Philadelphia home, a human-interest item chronicled the plight of the homeless in their city.

"Mom! Dad! Did you know there are people who don't have any home?"

"Yes, Trevor, there are, even here in Philadelphia. Isn't it sad?" his parents responded.

"We've got to do something, and we've got to do it *right now!*" the boy announced.

The night was cold and Trevor's home was cozy and comfortable. "Maybe we could do something tomorrow . . . or we can give to the homeless through our church's mission budget," Trevor's mother soothed. A dejected Trevor shuffled off to his bedroom, depressed by his parents' obtuseness.

Mom and dad sensed their son's hurting, sympathetic heart, so they talked after Trevor left. They knew that their son had just learned about loving in Sunday school and that he was trying to share that love. How could they stifle that rare and precious impulse?

"Trevor," they called, "Get your coat. We'll take you downtown and we'll find some homeless people."

Trevor dashed to his bed and scooped his favorite pillow into his arms and the yellow blanket that warmed him each night. Then armed with the best he knew about warmth and comfort, Trevor rode with his parents into the inner city, looking for someone cold and homeless.

"I see somebody!" Trevor shouted. A shadowed figure huddled over a sidewalk grate seeking the warmth from the subways that passed underneath. Dad pulled to the curb and Trevor jumped out, the yellow blanket in his arms.

"Mom, give me the pillow, too." Trevor handed the blanket and pillow to the man shivering on the grating.

"Thank you, son." The man smiled at Trevor as he wrapped himself in his new treasures.

During the ride home Trevor, with shining eyes, asked repeatedly, "Did you see how that man smiled?" Trevor's loving sympathy blossomed into his compulsion to serve.

Portrait of a Servant

People like Trevor are few in today's world. The concept of serving has slipped from the scene as stealthily as a snake slithers off a footpath. Yet Jesus demonstrated serving in the final hours before his crucifixion and he told us to follow his example. It's an absolute for us who call ourselves Christians.

Remember reading, when you first began this book, the story of how Jesus washed the feet of his disciples? That same story crops up again as we learn about serving. (Wonder how many lessons we could learn from those few paragraphs?)

Jesus didn't preach to his men about becoming servants; instead, he *showed them how* as he, their teacher and leader, performed the humble rites of hospitality. "This is how my followers should act," he was saying by example. "This is how I show my love to you. Imitate me."

Play the video of that scene in your imagination. What you see as you watch the Master bend over the dusty feet of his friends is the perfect portrait of a servant.

Jesus knew that only hours away death awaited him, the humiliating, agonizing death of a criminal. He had already told his men (John 12:23–24) that he was going to die, but he spoke of it as the time for him to be glorified. It makes you wonder whether they comprehended even a fraction of his meaning. We never call death a "glory," do we?

Jesus also knew that his death, his time of glorification, meant that he would leave earth and his disciples. This was his final chance to teach them an important lesson, one, since it was the last experience they would share with him, that would burn within them for the rest of their lives.

Jesus was aware that Satan, our evil enemy, lurked in that room, doing his best to undermine God's plan to save the world through the sacrifice of his Son.

"The devil had already prompted Judas Iscariot . . . to betray Jesus" (13:2).

The superhuman scope of Jesus' knowledge must have wearied him severely, and yet his driving motivation at that crucial moment was love. He loved those twelve even while they bickered among themselves as he tried to tell them of his death and departure.

Bickered? Oh, yes.

The problem? Who would be the greatest. Leonardo da Vinci didn't catch that moment in his gentle, benign portrayal of the Last Supper, did he? But in Luke 22:24–27 the writer says that they were disputing about "which of them was considered to be greatest." Jesus patiently pointed out to them one more time how believers are to view these issues.

"Who is greater," he asks, "the one who is at the table or the one who serves?"

That was easy. Custom, culture, and human behavior had taught them that greatness is enjoyed by the one who receives the service of others. Servants are nothing. But listen! He goes on.

"But I am among you as one who serves." The Christ who claimed to be the Son of God—King of kings and Lord of lords the Bible calls him—*serves*.

Luke gave us Christ's words regarding serving, and John wrote about his example of washing feet. In either case, because they needed to know what he could teach them, Jesus ignored the men's peripheral problems and stuck to the issue he sought to make clear for them.

His love extended to all his disciples in spite of Judas' plan to betray him to the Jewish officials who wanted Jesus out of the way. He didn't by-pass Judas as he circled the room washing, drying, loving. Even though it must have cost him dearly, he struggled to communicate an absolute truth: He that is greatest must be servant of all.

If serving is part of following Jesus, of being like him, what can we learn from this example he left for us? Let's freeze-frame the video step by step and discover what's there for us.

Position of the Servant

First, John 13:4 tells us that Jesus rose from the table and left his place of honor. Again, Leonardo's depiction notwithstanding, the disciples sat on pillows around a U-shaped, foot-high table (more reclining than sitting), with feet aimed away from the table.

Jesus, the Master, sat in the curve of the U, the place of honor, his due as teacher and leader. The disciples bickered among themselves, arguing about their potential for power and authority. Of course none of them thought of helping the others to ease and refreshment by washing their feet clean of the dust of the road. That was the job of household slaves or servants. But in this borrowed room, no slaves attended them. Anything hospitable had to be done one to another.

So the man who was about to die rose and left his place of honor—in the same way he left his place with God in heaven—to serve those he loved.

The second thing Jesus did was to remove his outer garment, probably a long-sleeved caftan-like article of clothing. Here's an interesting and illuminating bit of information. The Greek word that speaks of Jesus' laying aside his robe appears also in John 10:15—"I lay down my life for the sheep."

He was modeling sacrifice, much more than offering a lesson in hospitality. Knowing that bit about the meaning of the word, however, might give the art of hospitality a new and powerful purpose.

Next, Jesus wrapped a towel around his waist as an apron of sorts, and in so doing identified himself as their servant. Paul wrote about this concept in Philippians 2:7–8. Jesus made himself nothing, "taking the very nature [or form] of a servant. . . . He humbled himself and became obedient to death— even death on a cross!"

Then Jesus poured water on his friends' feet, just as he would pour out his blood on the cross for those same friends and for us who read these pages and for the whole world.

In the pouring of water (and of blood) Jesus washed away the dirt of the road from feet (and life's sin dirt from the hearts of those who accept him). In 1 John 1:7 the apostle says, "The blood of Jesus, [God's] Son, purifies us from all sin."

Then when he finished washing twelve pairs of dirty feet, Jesus resumed his place at the head of the table. Continuing the comparison of what Jesus did that day before their last meal together with what he's done for us through his life, death, and resurrection, Hebrews 1:3 says it best: "After he had provided purification for sins, he sat down at the right hand of the Majesty in heaven."

Protest of a Prideful Disciple

While Jesus was teaching the concept of service, Simon Peter blurted out a noisy protest.

"Lord, are you going to wash my feet?"

"You do not realize now what I am doing, but later you will understand," Jesus replied.

"No," said Peter, "you shall never wash my feet."

Peter's pullback from Jesus' attempt to wash his feet was not humility, but the protest of a prideful disciple. Peter felt insulted that his rabbi, his respected teacher, would lower himself to such menial chores before a roomful of his peers. In the same way, Peter hated to hear the Master talk about dying when he wanted him to take over the kingdom with a triumphal, dramatic flourish. How can one born to rule die before he is crowned?

Jesus' reply to that was, "Get behind me, Satan." He would not be tempted with ideas of greatness. His concept of greatness differed sharply from theirs. Peter liked being associated with the man in charge, the master, the future king. By means of this liaison, that which was beneath the lofty one would also be beneath his cohorts (including Peter), definitely a pleasant prospect.

But Jesus shattered that air castle by knotting a towel around his waist and splashing water over Peter's feet.

At this point another dimension enters in. For some of us it is much easier to do for others than to allow them to do for us. That may have been part of Peter's problem, too. If Jesus had ordered him to serve his fellow disciples or himself in some way, Peter might have moved reluctantly toward the task, but it would have been easier than to sit in his place and allow the Master to wash his feet.

When I (Vicki) was recuperating from surgery, I struggled against the idea that I must depend on others to care for my home, my children, even many of my own needs. As people cleaned my house, cooked my family's food, and entertained my children, God broke through my resistance and spoke.

"These people find joy in serving you. But, Vicki, your pride is getting in the way and blinding you to what is happening for them."

Serving is a two-way street; at times we serve, at other times we accept the service of others. This fact reminds me (Carroll) of an experience I had as a junior missionary in Korea.

Ella Ruth, my co-worker, invited me to go with her to a home for blind and orphaned young women. She was serving them in practical ways, one of which was to help them learn skills by which they could support themselves.

We toured around their humble little compound, squeezed their hands and hugged those handicapped girls who had neither parent nor relative to care what became of them. They all knew Ella Ruth because of her regular visits and her concern that they have shelter, food, and warm clothes.

One of the girls came to Ella Ruth and pushed into her hands a shopping bag made of plastic cord, one of the items they were making to sell in their efforts to move toward self-support. Ella Ruth knew that to accept the gift meant the girl would sacrifice several pennies' worth of necessities.

"Oh, no," she cried. "You need to sell this. You need the money."

But the girl wouldn't budge. She held Ella Ruth's hands closed around the bag. "Receive it," she insisted. "I want you to, please. *I've never had anyone to give a gift to before.*"

So Ella Ruth served the blind orphan girl by accepting her gift, sensing how it added to the girl's sense of self-worth by having at last a loved one to give to.

Let's return to the story. Why did Jesus wash the feet of his friends?

Purpose of Serving

First, he wanted to teach humility, that unless they could accept and assume leastness, lowliness, they could never achieve greatness. In verses 14, 15, and 16 he said "I, your Lord and Teacher, have washed your feet, you also should wash one another's feet. I have set you an example . . . no servant is greater than his master."

Jesus also wanted them to learn about forgiveness. This crops up in the conversation between Peter and Jesus beginning at verse 9. After Jesus insisted that he must wash Peter's feet, Peter decides to plunge in entirely.

"Then, Lord," he said, "not just my feet but my hands and my head as well!"

"A person who has had a bath," Jesus answered, "needs only to wash his feet; his whole body is clean."

Jesus was saying, "You have been cleansed. Your sins are forgiven." He moved in his meaning from physical matters to those of the spirit. When we repent of our sins and invite Jesus into our lives, to make us Christians, we are not automatically perfect. We still manage to dirty our feet along the way. When we do we must seek forgiveness and ask the Master to wash our soiled feet.

This is what makes 1 John 2:1 so beautiful. John writes, "But if anybody does sin, we have one who speaks to the Father in our defense—Jesus Christ, the Righteous One." Read also 1 John 1:9; Galatians 6:1–2; and Ephesians 4:32.

Jesus was teaching his followers, all of us, how to stay clean along the way. The disciples must have caught a new dimension in their understanding of forgiveness as they reflected on that night and its events. They realized that Jesus knew what Judas was going to do to him, yet he washed the betrayer's feet along with everyone else's. Now *that's* forgiveness!

Another lesson Jesus taught regarding serving is that there is blessing for the servant. "Now that you know these things, you will be blessed if you do them" (v. 17).

Jesus had already told them they must follow his example. Perhaps the men thought that now they should wash Jesus' feet, and that would've been all right. He was the Master, after all, and they his disciples.

But he wasn't thinking of their serving him; he was soon to return to the Father in heaven. Instead, he intended that they serve each other and in that way serve him. But how could he expect these competitive individualists who had just been arguing over place to bend, to stoop, to serve?

Irrational? Certainly. But he expects this of all of us who follow him. It's an absolute of the Christian way; if we want to serve the Master whom we're learning to love so deeply, we must do so by serving each other.

When we do, riches of the spirit await us. So it

says in Ephesians 6:7. Serve, it says, as if you were serving the Lord. And speaking of blessing, check John 12:26. "My Father," Jesus said, "will honor the one who serves me."

Mother Teresa, Nobel prize-winning missionary to India, once shared the prayer used by her associates as they face each day filled with sick and dying people. It goes like this: "Dearest Lord, may I see you today and every day in the person of your sick, your poor, and whilst nursing them, minister to You. Though You hide yourself behind the unattractive disguise of the irritable, the exacting, may I still recognize You and say, 'Jesus, my patient, how sweet it is to be serving You.'"[1]

Look at others through Jesus' eyes. See them as the Lord and yourself as ministering to him. When we do this, it transforms our perspective on the business of serving.

Virtue magazine reported that a TV interviewer once asked Mother Teresa about her work among the wretched and the dying.

"Don't you get discouraged sometimes? No matter how hard you work, millions still suffer and die without help."

"Oh, no," the little woman replied, "I don't grow discouraged. You see, I do not count the way you do, by the thousands. I count the way God counts; I count one by one, the ones we have rescued."[2]

Satan wants us to think we can never finish the job of serving in Jesus' name since there are so many who need him, so let's give up. We can't do it all. But he is the enemy and his perspective opposes God's. God wants us to look on each opportunity to serve as sent from him. He wants us to count by ones, faithfully serving in the Master's name. And God not only helps us count by ones but often takes our ones and multiplies them into tens, hundreds, thousands, or more.

Trevor's nighttime trek into midtown Philadelphia affected his viewpoint permanently. It took place years ago, and today a network of caring exists all across the USA because of it. A 33-room hotel called "Trevor's Place" shelters and feeds men and women who need its hospitality. Fourteen chapters of Trevor's campaign for the homeless reach out and serve in love.

A food-run for street people feeds over 150 each day–365 days a year. A twenty-four-hour day-care center and home for mothers and their children called Next Door (because it was a former convent next door to Trevor's Place) recently opened its doors. A large thrift shop provides for the needs of the underprivileged of West Philadelphia. And over twenty chapters of Trevor's Campaign for the Homeless reach out and serve in love.[3] His persistence is sensitizing more and more people to the plight of the homeless in city doorways, under bridges, and over subway grates.

Loving service assumes multiple forms, from pouring tea to the pouring out of one's whole life, in the Master's name. The important thing is to do it.

*   *   *

Lord Jesus, make me see your towel-wrapped body and ministering hands as I dash through my day. Open my eyes to opportunities to serve that lie within my reach, and if you want me to reach even further than I ever have before, keep prodding me until I do what you want me to do.

What Do You Think?

1. What tasks do you consider menial or low-down? What do you do about them?

2. How can you serve so that it would be equivalent to washing someone's feet? (Read Gal. 6:1–2; Eph. 4:32.)

3. Read John 12:1–8. Why did Mary do what she did?

4. How did the others react to her behavior?

5. How did Jesus respond?

Notes

[1]Mother Teresa, "The Joy of Loving," *Virtue* 7, no. 4 (December 1984), 25.
[2]Ibid.
[3]Information provided by Trevor's Campaign for the Homeless, P.O. Box 21, Gladwyne, PA 19035.

7

remain

Read John 15:1–11

WHEN CHARLES and I (Vicki) lived in Australia we visited a vineyard near the Murray River. Since fresh fruit and vegetables are a passion with me, I felt I was in heaven as I gazed across acres and acres of vines drooping with fat, luscious grapes. While I stared, our hosts talked about the hours of labor required to bring those picture-perfect vines to continued fruitful production. Whenever I read John 15, I remember their description of what is needed to persuade those vines to produce the grapes I enjoy so much.

In this section of Scripture, Jesus continues his explanation of how Christians should live and behave by talking about vines. Read the first eleven verses.

Finished? Again Jesus speaks in figurative forms to convey truth. Perhaps he and his friends had left the room where he washed their feet and were walking along the road, talking as they went. He knew his teaching time with them was over so he strove to cram final pieces of information into their minds. Thus they would be available for recall after he was gone. Maybe one of the disciples drew their attention to a flourishing grapevine heavy with fruit like the ones in Australia. Jesus seized the moment to reinforce his teaching. He knew that in the years to come they would desperately need wisdom for leadership far beyond their capabilities.

"I am the true vine," Jesus told them. "My Father [God] is the gardener."

And he went on to talk about what they already knew—gardeners must prune and trim and train before the vines can do what they are created to do— bear fruit. What all believers should learn from these verses is that we are to undergo pruning, an uncomfortable prospect, so we will bear spiritual fruit in order to react as Jesus would in every situation life tosses at us.

Jesus' life, which we learn about by reading Matthew, Mark, Luke, and John, is a series of encounters and experiences in which he acted at times with incredible wisdom or restraint. Picture that night in the Garden of Gethsemane. Matthew wrote that Jesus had gone there to pray, asking the disciples to pray with him. They fell asleep, abandoning him to his lonely agonies. When he finished, Jesus woke them with a gentle reproach as he turned to face betrayal and death.

"Rise, let us go," he said. "Here comes my betrayer!"

Judas stepped out of the shadows even as Jesus spoke, followed by an armed crowd. He walked up to the Master and kissed him, crying, "Greetings, Rabbi!"

"Friend, do what you came for," Jesus said to Judas. Then the crowd of men surged forward and arrested Jesus, who spoke not one word about justice, his rights, or the betrayal of his "friend" Judas.

Other times Jesus seized the initiative with courage and boldness that could have been called foolhardy. Even though the Jewish officials and religious leaders plotted against him, Jesus strode toward Jerusalem, entering the city to the cheers of the people as he rode a borrowed donkey.

As if that weren't enough, he went into the temple and found it clotted with profiteers exchanging money and selling sacrificial birds and animals. Imagine the fury on his face as he upturned tables, sending stacks of coins bouncing and clinking across the stone floors. Imagine the cries of protest when he smashed the cages that held cooing doves, setting them free, and destroying the profits of their keepers.

"It is written," he shouted, " 'My house will be called a house of prayer' [Isaiah 56:7], but you are making it a 'den of robbers' " (Jeremiah 7:11).

Does living a fruitful Christian life mean measuring up to that? Let's dig around and see what we can find out.

Command To Bear Fruit

"Bear much fruit, showing yourselves to be my disciples" (v. 8). Jesus' followers must bear fruit, no question. He says so here. This kind of spiritual production is not an option; it is required of us as Christians.

Back in Matthew 3:8, John the Baptist, in his ministry of preparation for Jesus' coming, eyed the religious leaders who joined the crowds trekking out to the desert to hear him preach and watch him baptize converts. "Repent!" he exhorted, but he knew that the Pharisees and Sadducees came only to criticize, so he spoke to them bluntly.

"Produce fruit," he ordered, "in keeping with repentance." Give evidence that your life is committed to God.

When Paul wrote to the Christians in Rome, he said that we belong to him who was raised from the dead (Jesus), "in order that we might bear fruit to God" (Rom. 7:4). Then he defines fruit-bearing more clearly in Colossians 1:10, saying that it is "bearing fruit in every good work, growing in the knowledge of God." So if a believer bears fruit, it means he does what is good and he grows and matures in his knowledge of God. And it is absolutely clear that this is part of our remaining in Jesus, the Vine.

Consideration of Fruit

When God talks to us through the Bible about bearing fruit, what does he mean? What kind of fruit? What are the spiritual equivalents of grapes, apples, oranges?

He wants evidence in our daily living that we remain in Christ and that he remains in us just as the vine grower wants proof that his pruning, fertilizing, and cultivating affect the vines under his care.

Two verses in Galatians 5 spell it out by giving us a

list of the kind of fruit the Lord looks for: love, joy, peace, patience, kindness, goodness, faithfulness, gentleness, and self-control (vv. 22–23).

"Live as children of light," Paul wrote in Ephesians 5, "(for the fruit of the light consists in all goodness, righteousness and truth) and find out what pleases the Lord" (vv. 8b–10).

Read that list aloud, beginning with love and ending with self-control. Then throw in goodness, righteousness, and truth for good measure. Daunting, isn't it? Wonderful, enviable qualities, but who can reach that high?

My (Carroll's) friend Eleanor had an artist paint that list of spiritual fruit on individual decorated plaques which she hung around her kitchen. They certainly kept the concept before her and everyone else who went there to lean on the counter and watch her work.

But the question remains, how does one become loving, gentle, good, kind, controlled? According to the Bible these qualities are expected of children of God, an absolute for Christian living. Is there also teaching to show us how we can reach such an impossible goal?

Conditions for Fruitfulness

Jesus said, "Remain in me." If we do, he will remain in us. It's all there in John 15:4. "No branch can bear fruit by itself; it must remain in the vine." And lest we miss the point, he says, "Neither can you bear fruit unless you remain in me."

So the first condition for fruitfulness is *to remain in Christ*. If a branch had the power to choose, it could not expect to bear fruit if it decided to strike out on its own. Its only hope for satisfying production is to stay part of the vine. To remain.

That's all well and good for the plant kingdom, you say, but how does a human being insure that he is plugged into God at all times? Get specific about remaining. How does it happen?

Three simple ways:

1. *Read the Bible.* Soak, saturate yourself in Scripture. "Find out what pleases the Lord," Paul says in Ephesians 5:10. The best way to find out what pleases him is to read his Word. It's all there.

2. *Pray.* We talked about this at length in the Ask chapter. Go back and review. Be sure you understand and accept the fact that prayer, this bond with God, is crucial to remaining in Christ. Remaining is crucial to fruit-bearing.

3. *Fellowship.* "Let us consider how we may spur one another on toward love and good deeds. Let us not give up meeting together . . . but let us encourage one another" (Heb. 10:24–25).

During the Brown County (Indiana) Women's Retreat recently, an encounter took place in my workshop (Vicki's) that proves the validity of the importance of fellowship. I was teaching Proverbs and assigned two questions for the participants to answer:

1. If God offered to give you anything tangible or material, for what would you ask?
2. If God would give you anything intangible or spiritual, what would you want from him?

After the workshop a young woman came to me and told me this story:

> I came to this retreat with a heavy heart. Just yesterday I said good-bye to my 69-year-old parents who returned to Haiti as missionaries. Because of political turmoil and violence there, we family members had to sign a release that we wouldn't hold the mission responsible if anything happened to Mom and Dad.
>
> When I shared with my group that my spiritual request of God was peace because of this situation with my parents, do you know what happened?
>
> The minute I spoke of my fears for my parents and my desire for peace from God, Linda, a woman in my group, became excited. She said, "We used to be missionaries in Haiti and via shortwave my husband talks with people there almost every day. He stays in touch with the political situation and can keep you informed about your parents."
>
> We exchanged phone numbers and Linda promised that she and her husband would keep us in touch with what is going on in Haiti. I came away from that time with *such peace*! Any day that I want to know what is happening, I can.

God used the fellowship encounter of those two women to bless and encourage, to spur each other on toward love and good deeds.

In another condition for fruitfulness it's a little harder to find blessing and encouragement because it requires us to allow the pruning process. In John 15 we've already learned that Jesus is the vine and God is the gardener. And the gardener cuts off every branch that bears no fruit. Okay, that's not too bad. But then he goes on in a less comfortable mode. "Every branch that does bear fruit he trims clean so that it will be even more fruitful." Ouch!

Korean hillsides are full of pear and apple orchards that lie bare and dormant through the long cold winter. But late in February or early in March, when the bark on the small branches is just beginning to blush with a rosy hue, workers move among the trees with clippers and saws. They lop and trim and cut on those awakening fruit trees, reducing them to gnarled, misshapen relics with only four or five branches left on the main trunk. To make it worse, they gather up all the bits and pieces they cut away and without a backward glance throw them onto a fire.

People are a little better off than trees because we can escape pruning if we want to. We don't stand rooted to a hillside unable to move. But those first five verses of John 15 suggest that remaining in Jesus is required for fruit bearing and he or she who remains will be pruned. (Maybe a review of the absolute of trust might encourage us at this point.)

And besides, what needs pruning out of my life anyway? What was wrong, for that matter, with all the branches the Korean gardeners trimmed from the apple trees?

Ever hear of suckers? Not the foolish people who can be taken advantage of, but the shoots that gardeners trim off because they do not produce fruit. Yet for their own existence they suck energy from plants that do bear fruit.

So what are the spiritual suckers that sap growth and vitality from Christian believers? Bitterness, rage, and anger, along with every form of malice are listed in Ephesians 4:31. "Get rid of these," Paul says. In Colossians 3:8–10 he adds to the list slander, filthy language, and lying. In 1 Peter 2:1 we read about deceit, hypocrisy, and envy.

A word of comfort comes in Hebrews 12 as we contemplate God's pruning away of this spiritual dead wood. "No discipline seems pleasant at the time, but painful. [You can say that again. Who wants to admit such traits grow on his tree, let alone submit to the cuts that remove them?] Later on, however, it produces a harvest of righteousness and peace for those who have been trained by it" (v. 11).

So it sounds as if our submission to God's pruning of the sin that destroys our spiritual productivity is not only essential but profitable as well. If we are to remain in him, we must allow him to keep us clean and fruitful.

Consequences of Fruitfulness

The first result of remaining attached to Christ the Vine is God's response to our praying. "If you remain in me and my words remain in you, ask whatever you wish, and it will be given you" (v. 7).

Living intimately with Christ and allowing his words and his will to saturate our spirits makes it almost impossible to ask God for anything that opposes his purposes. So when we pray we'll be seeking his desires and making them our own; consequently, we ask whatever we wish (he wishes) and it is given us.

Further, when we bear spiritual fruit or evidence the characteristics listed earlier, we honor God the Father. We glorify him, it says in verse 8. Disciples who live and act as the Lord has taught them to honor their Teacher.

When I (Carroll) was a little girl, I lived with my family on a farm in central Ohio. People from other places often came by to visit because my father was an itinerant evangelist who made friends wherever he went. Happy were the times when Daddy would turn to my brother and me after the guests departed and share a compliment he'd received from them.

"The Joneses (or the Smiths) remarked about your obedience and your good behavior," he would say. "Thank you for being so helpful (or so quiet, or for washing dishes while the adults talked)."

Daddy and Mother let us know that our living out their teaching before our visitors had brought compliments and good words to them. They were pleased, and because they were, so were we.

Consistent love and obedience to God, evidence of our remaining in him, bring joy. Verse 11 speaks of his joy filling us, and when it does, our joy is complete, lacking nothing.

Then, full of joy, obedient to God's direction, and freed of the evil suckers that sap our spiritual vitality, we can stand before the Lord with a clear conscience. This is brought out in 1 John 2:28: "And now, dear children, continue [remain, abide] in him, so that when he appears we may be confident and unashamed before him at his coming."

The Bible teaches us that Jesus will return to earth some day, and he will call upon us to account for the way we've lived. Can you imagine what it will be like to stand before Almighty God and explain the dids and did-nots of your life? Whew! If we remain in him, this verse tells us, we can stand before him confident and unashamed, knowing that we centered our existence on his principles and sought to honor him in every circumstance.

Consequences of Fruitfulness

"If anyone does not remain in me, he is like a branch that is thrown away and withers; such branches are picked up, thrown into the fire and burned" (v. 6).

Hard words! It's an unpleasant thought that unproductive branches end up tossed out and burned. But if we believe in the Lord Jesus, if we trust him and seek to obey him, then we'll accept what he told and re-told us in John 15, that he expects us to remain in him, to stick as close to him as a branch clings to its parent vine. We'll believe that he means what he says when he tells us that those who do not cannot survive.

Now we can struggle and twist and try out explanations as to what God literally means, and he does express himself clearly elsewhere in the Bible about punishment for disbelief and disobedience. But in this instance the far more important factor is the positive one: all the blessings and benefits that come to the one who remains, who endures and benefits from pruning, who bears fruit.

It's like those trees in the Korean orchards. Not too many weeks after their ordeal with the saws and clippers, the branches that remain burst into gorgeous bloom, painting the hillsides with translucent shimmering white and pink. And then late in summer and on into autumn as apples and pears grow heavy on those fruitful branches, the men come back. No cutting tools this time, but they gently support the heavy branches with notched sticks and knotted cords. They even make paper pouches to put around the finest fruit to protect it from insects and disease.

The finished product, then, is ripe and delicious fruit—red apples and yellow pears—perfect! Which shows us what God has in mind when he urges us through the words of Jesus to remain in him first of all, then to produce fruit that honors him and blesses the world in which we live.

*   *   *

Lord, I like the idea of remaining in you. It makes me feel secure and loved, safe somehow. I don't like the pruning nearly so well, although I can see how lying, slander, malice, bitterness, and anger can detract from the evidence in my life that I belong to you.

So help me, Lord, not to squirm away from your pruning. Make my fruit production an honor to your name, for Jesus' sake.

What Do You Think?

1. Who is the gardener in John 15 and what are his responsibilities? In what ways has he worked or is now working in your life?

2. What is the purpose of pruning, both in gardening and in spiritual terms?

3. Why is it important to bear fruit?

4. What happens to fruitless branches?

5. What are we promised if we remain in Christ and his words remain in us?

8
witness

Read John 15:26–27 and
Acts 8:1–8; 26–40

PHILIP STOOD in the doorway squinting against the sunlight. "Where do you want me to go today, Lord?" he prayed. "Back to the marketplace? Beyond the city gate? What about the inns along the wall?"

"Go south to the road—the desert road—that goes down from Jerusalem to Gaza."

As Philip listened to the directions, he knew that they came from a messenger of God. Accustomed to such unexplained orders, he turned to take a drink of water from the jug standing in the shade of the house, then walked with long strides toward the desert road.

Philip had adapted to life in Samaria, if you can call his survival-based lifestyle adaptation. He cared little for clothes or food of fine quality. He slept in his small borrowed room only when his weary body refused to move further. He had come here to tell

Samaritans about the Master and had given himself
relentlessly to his task.

As the evangelist walked the desert road, he heard
the creak of chariot wheels. He stopped, turned, and
shading his eyes against the glare, looked back to see
who approached.

"Is this why I am here, Lord? If so, make me
ready," he breathed.

The chariot slowly drew abreast of Philip. He
could see that it was making a leisurely journey,
transporting a man of importance as comfortably as
the rocky road would allow. The passenger, Philip
learned from the banners borne by the chariot's
outriders, was an official of the Ethiopian court who
sat reading under a silken sunshade.

"Go to that chariot and stay near it," whispered
Philip's guiding voice.

Philip trotted alongside the slow-moving chariot.
The Ethiopian was reading aloud from the Jewish
prophet, Isaiah. Without bothering with greetings,
Philip spoke to the man.

"Do you understand what you are reading?"

The Ethiopian dropped the scroll into his lap and
looked over the chariot wheel at the man jogging
alongside. "How can I," he asked, "unless someone
explains it to me? Come up and sit with me and let
us talk about it."

Witnessing. Testifying. Gossiping the gospel,
some call it. Whatever term we use, telling the good
news about Jesus Christ is an absolute for those of us
who follow him; which is why Philip was living in a
foreign place and telling everyone he could about his
Savior.

"When the Counselor [the Holy Spirit] comes . . .

he will testify about me," Jesus said just before his crucifixion, "but you also must testify, for you have been with me from the beginning" (15:26–27).

Then Jesus was killed and a couple of days later returned from death. Just before he disappeared into heaven the Master turned aside his disciples' questions about the restoration of the kingdom here on earth, telling them that such things were not for them to know, for they are controlled by God.

"But you will receive power when the Holy Spirit comes upon you," he said, "and you will be my witnesses in Jerusalem, and in all Judea and Samaria, and to the ends of the earth" (Acts 1:8).

That is why Philip was in Samaria, to tell his traditional enemies about Jesus. At first all of Christ's followers huddled in Jerusalem, telling their story and winning many to faith in God's Son. But then nervousness among Jewish leaders about the Christians' activities exploded into hostility and fear. Avid, open persecution flared against Jesus' followers, scattering them across Judea and into Samaria.

Through this persecution Jesus' words came true. "You will be my witnesses in Jerusalem [where they earned beatings, stonings, and prison terms along with thousands of converts], and in all Judea and Samaria [where they fled to survive]." So it appears that Jesus knew what he was talking about. He used the pain of persecution to spread across the countryside the good news that salvation is available to everyone who trusts in the Christ.

Trained To Serve

Philip (not one of the original twelve) had been trained in Jerusalem and elected by his fellow

Christians along with six others to help to care for needy widows. He worked alongside Stephen whose martyr death triggered persecution against Jesus' followers.

Philip's leaving Jerusalem for Samaria as a witness, an evangelist, is a major tribute to the power of the Holy Spirit. Jews bore a longstanding hostility against Samaritans for intermarrying with local people who did not worship the one true God, thereby corrupting their religious practices and disobeying the guidelines given to Jews centuries before.

So Philip proclaimed Christ among people with whom he would have no relationship traditionally. But when the crowds heard him and felt the power of his words, "they all paid close attention to what he said" (Acts 8:6). The spiritual freedom that accompanied their acceptance of Philip's witness brought great joy to that city.

Obviously this was the Lord's plan for now, that Jesus' followers should witness about him to all peoples—even beyond sacred Jerusalem, and even to Samaritans.

Seeking the Spirit's Guidance

Don't you find it interesting that a Jewish evangelist whose nation held a special relationship with God could spend his time witnessing to Samaritans and Ethiopians, people far removed from his traditions?

Philip asked the Holy Spirit for guidance and he received it. "Go south to the road," came the directive. Philip obeyed. Then on the desert road the

Spirit spoke again. "Go to that chariot and stay near it."

As Philip moved alongside the chariot and heard the Ethiopian reading Isaiah's prophecy about the Messiah, he opened up the conversation in the most natural way possible. "Do you understand what you are reading?"

"How can I," the frustrated seeker responded, "unless someone explains it to me?"

His invitation to Philip to sit with him and talk about Scripture was no coincidence. The Holy Spirit did not create this encounter and then walk off and leave it like some windup toy abandoned on the floor. Since our witnessing is God's plan for telling the world about his love, the Holy Spirit's job is to enable those who are to do the telling.

"Tell me, please, who is the prophet talking about, himself or someone else?" the Ethiopian asked the Jew. And Philip began with the Christ-revealing verses in Isaiah (53:7–8) to tell his companion the good news about Jesus.

Charlie, who is a present-day witness for Christ is much like Philip. He travels regularly by air and often shares his faith with the person sitting next to him. Not only does he talk about it, but time and time again his talking results in someone praying over the roar of jet engines to receive Jesus as Savior, as did Philip's Ethiopian.

We lived next door to Charlie, and one day I (Vicki) asked him his secret. "Do you have a prepared question to ask that makes this happen all the time?"

"My secret is this," Charlie said. "Before I board any plane I ask the Lord to put me beside someone who is ripe and ready to receive him. Let me sit, I ask, by someone ready to respond because I don't want to waste the Lord's time or mine with someone unreceptive to Jesus.

"So I board the plane and enjoy watching people come down the aisle. I can usually tell who is going to sit by me. It's the person with the most miserable expression on his face."

Charlie's success in talking about Jesus and leading others to know him lies not in a formula approach, but in his asking the Holy Spirit to direct him to the person ready and hungry for a Savior.

Neither Philip nor Charlie nor any of us could witness with any effect without the Holy Spirit's aid. Why? Four reasons for starters.

1. The Spirit convicts. He is the one who does the work, who points out the human need for a Savior. He tells the ones to whom we speak that this truth will change their lives. Don't ever be fooled into thinking that we do it, no matter how great our satisfaction at seeing someone to whom we've spoken accept him (John 16:8–10; 15:26).

2. The Spirit renews. He does the changing, the transforming from sinner to servant of the Lord Jesus (Rom. 8:1–2, 6, 11; 2 Cor. 3:17–18).

3. The Spirit assures. He communicates to each believer that he belongs to God and is free from condemnation (Rom. 8:15–17).

4. The Spirit equips. He gives us the skill to witness, to talk about Jesus whenever and wherever we should, even when we're anxious. When the time comes, we step aside and let the Spirit lead just as Philip did out on the desert road (1 Cor. 12:7–11; Mark 13:10–11).

Sensing Needs

Sensitivity is crucial to witnessing about our faith in Jesus. We must sense the need of the person to whom we speak and then address that need. Jesus felt the needs of the people who surrounded him, which is why he fed hungry crowds and then told them he was the bread of life; why he discussed thirst with a woman who'd come to draw water from a well, telling her he was the source of living water. In the same way, Jesus readily forgave a woman who writhed in shame over her sin of adultery.

Philip exhibited the same sensitive spirit when he overheard the Ethiopian official reading Scripture. "Here is a man hungry for God," he must have thought. So he opened a discussion about the writings of Isaiah, plugging in where the man's need evidenced itself.

I (Vicki) wish I'd been more sensitive when I held the door for an elderly woman trying to enter our shopping mall. We chatted long enough for me to discover that she had just recovered from pneumonia and still felt wobbly and uncertain on her feet. She seemed lonely but I was rushing to meet a friend for lunch.

"You take care now," I tossed over my shoulder as I left her inside the door. "Don't try to do too much."

I lunched with my friend and dashed through the remainder of my day but the lady at the door haunted me. She haunts me still. My guiding voice deep inside me says the dear lady might have needed to know the love of Jesus. Had I been more sensitive and willing to forego a bowl of soup, perhaps she would have joined the family of God. But my sensitivity was late in coming, too late for that woman. I'm praying that next time I'll be less driven and more alert.

Seizing Opportunities

Philip not only sensed the Ethiopian's need, but he also used good communication skills to persuade the man to open up about his need. Rather than seizing the man by the front of his robe and launching into a sermon about repentance, Philip asked him a question designed to open doors to dialogue.

"Do you understand what you are reading?"

Not being Jewish and perhaps new to Jewish Scriptures, the Ethiopian hadn't a clue to their meaning. All he knew was a deep unrest, an undefined dissatisfaction (maybe he did not recognize it as a hunger for God, yet maybe by reading the scroll he hoped to satisfy whatever gnawed at him).

Along with questions that cause a person to open up about his search or his feelings are casual comments we believers can make that might stimulate reactions from our hearers.

We can offer to pray when someone is explaining or complaining about difficulties or disappointments. Or when the conversation turns to fitness and aerobics, if appropriate, you might say, "I do aerobics at my Bible class." That ought to stimulate some interest, or at least curiosity.

But avoid clichés. Maybe by now you've been around Christians and church long enough that you speak the lingo, the jargon that communicates spiritual meaning to us who believe but doesn't say anything to the uninitiated. Try to find fresh ways to say "born again" or "justified," "redeemed," and "saved." To "approach the throne of grace" to you means praying, but someone else might think that you used to be on speaking terms with the late Princess of Monaco (remember Princess Grace?). For people steeped in Scripture these and others all carry powerful, personal meaning, but for others they may be only amusing or, worse, bewildering.

Another communication tool for witnessing is to anticipate defenses that skeptics and nonbelievers throw up against faith in God. You can anticipate a standard excuse by saying, "There are many hypocrites in the church and that really bothers me. But what bothers me more is that many people don't understand what a *real* Christian is."

That should start the talk flowing.

Be sure, however, that you have fixed in your mind what a real Christian is; more, be sure you are one before you seek to persuade a friend to try it.

Spotlighting Jesus

Notice Philip's starting point when he witnessed to the Ethiopian. He began with Jesus Christ. Acts 8:35 says that Philip picked up on the Scripture the Ethiopian was reading and explained the good news—not about what a wonderful church he attended, nor how much satisfaction he enjoyed in social work, but pointed the seeker to Jesus.

I (Carroll) sat beside a young Chinese businessman named Tai Seng on a flight from Singapore to Manila. When he discovered that I am a Christian, he wanted to discuss religion. Early on he asked me,

"Do you see any value in religions other than Christianity?"

I gulped, knowing I was over my head. But I also knew the Holy Spirit would fill my mouth with the right words if only I were willing to open it.

"Yes," I answered, "many of the world's religions offer some good teaching about peace and love and self-sacrifice. But only Christianity introduces us to Jesus, telling us that he is God's Son and letting us know how God sent him to build a bridge between us and our Creator."

Focus on Jesus from the beginning and you can't go wrong. By the way, eventually Tai Seng and his wife accepted Christ and were baptized in their own swimming pool.

That's all well and good, you may be saying about now, for a missionary flying around the world, or for a mature Christian like Charlie with a sales background, or for Philip who was pushed out by danger and persecution. But me? I'm shy, or I'm young, or I just found Jesus myself so I'm spiritually immature.

Of course you are. You're you, created and loved by God. He doesn't expect you to be Philip or Charlie. He wants you to be you, but that means you at your best. And we've discovered in these pages that Scripture tells us that God expects us, whoever we are, to tell others about him, an absolute for the Christian way. People live and move within your sphere of influence, which only you can touch—not Charlie, not even Billy Graham, only you.

Read 1 Peter 3:15–17. It tells us to be ready: "Always be prepared to give an answer to everyone who asks you to give the reason for the hope that you have." So get ready. Soak in Scripture. Read the

Gospels (Matthew, Mark, Luke, and John) until you know Jesus well and can talk about him with enthusiasm and authority.

Then ask God to free you from shame and embarrassment about your faith. Aim for the freedom Paul enjoyed so he could write in Romans 1:16, "I am not ashamed of the gospel."

When I (Carroll) was a teenager, I *was* ashamed of the gospel. I dreaded the possibility that anyone of my peers might discover that I was a Christian and perhaps different from them. This was a dreadful period in my life and I'm thankful it's behind me.

Once you break free of the bondage of reticence to talk about your faith, the Lord can fill you with exuberance and pleasure at finding chances to witness about him. Now I rather enjoy being different and find that my peculiarities can open dialogue with people and shift the spotlight to Jesus.

Back in Acts 4:20 we read that even though Peter and John had been jailed, tried, and ordered not to talk about him, they replied to their tormenters, "We cannot help speaking about what we have seen and heard." They were not talking about big fish they'd caught or strange towns they'd visited. They were so filled with the joy and excitement of knowing the Lord Jesus, and so freed from timidity and reticence to acknowledge his presence in their lives that they spoke of him non-stop.

So begin where you are. If you have never been imprisoned for your faith, don't feel you must wait until you have before you can say something worthwhile about the Master. If you work with your hands, don't think you must go to seminary before you can acknowledge that belief and trust and love for Jesus are important to you. Ask the Holy Spirit to unlock your jaws and gild your tongue with joyous, winsome words about the Lord.

Open your mind and heart, then, to what else Jesus said about witnessing. Remember Acts 1:8? "You will receive power," it says, "when the Holy Spirit comes on you; and you will be my witnesses in Jerusalem [they told about Jesus in that city until persecution clamped down, didn't they?], and in all Judea and Samaria [Philip took action in Samaria], *and to the ends of the earth*" (emphasis ours).

Out there beyond our country's borders wait billions of people, God's beloved people, who still don't know who he is, who don't know he sent Jesus to bridge the gap between him and them. God has no other plan to let them know but that we tell them. This has to be the reason that Jesus' last words to his twelve friends, and us, were an order to take to the world our information and experiences.

Along with his order in Acts to witness to the ends of the earth, Luke writes in chapter 24 how Jesus talked to them just before he returned to heaven and told them how they were to spread the word. "Repentance and forgiveness of sins will be preached . . . to all nations, beginning at Jerusalem" (v. 47).

Mark wrote about Jesus' last moments with the disciples in chapter 16. "Go into all the world," he quotes the Master as saying, "and preach the good news to all creation" (v. 15).

Matthew recorded similar words that he heard on the Galilean mountain where Jesus had told his disciples to meet him. "Go and make disciples of all nations, baptizing them in the name of the Father and of the Son and of the Holy Spirit, and teaching them to obey everything I have commanded you. And surely I am with you always, to the very end of the age" (28:18–20).

Jesus made absolutely clear through the writings of several witnesses that he planned for us, his followers, to tell the whole world about himself. This is not an option; reaching out to his waiting world must be included in our witnessing.

"What does that mean?" you ask. "Must I dump everything and board a plane for Indonesia or Africa?"

Maybe. Thousands have done just that at God's direction. If that is what he wants you to do, you'd better do it, secure in the knowledge that he's promised to be with you. Countless missionaries have staked their lives on that promise and have planted flourishing communities of Christians around the globe because of the Lord's faithfulness.

However, the Lord does not allow every one of his children the privilege of serving full time overseas as missionaries. How, then, does someone who wants to obey Jesus' final order do so from home? Can we share his good news to the ends of the earth without making it a career?

Sure we can. Every Christian can and should do something. Does your church have any kind of missions outreach program? Learn about it. Discover the kinds of ministry that are promoted and supported by your fellowship. Let's hope people are involved in those ministries, people for whom you can pray. Get acquainted with those missionaries and with their co-workers, local Christian leaders who are native to the region and are perhaps products of the witnessing carried out by the sent ones.

Even if you don't switch careers and become a professional missionary, opportunities abound for you to join a guided tour to visit mission work. Spend your vacation money on a trip to Haiti or Ecuador or Korea to see what God is doing in those places. You'll meet missionaries and local believers, maybe even help them in their witnessing for a few days.

Persecution may never force you into involvement with different nationalities as it did for Philip. But remember, the most important thing about Philip's ministry in Samaria and with the Ethiopian was his obedience to God's voice. You already know that Jesus directed us to involve ourselves in witnessing at home and around the world. So all that remains is to find out where and when and how.

*   *   *

Lord Jesus, it mystifies me that you depend on us, your wobbly, sometimes wayward followers, to tell the world you love it. Yet rather than argue the point, I ask you to show me my part in doing it. And as I obey the other absolutes I'm learning about, give me what I need for this one, too. I want to tell my near neighbors about you, and I want to help people on the other side of the world to discover your love. Teach me how to go about it.

What Do You Think?

Read John 15:26–27

1. What did Jesus tell the disciples they must do?

2. Why were they qualified to do this? Am I qualified?

Read Psalms 66:16 and 71:15; Isaiah 63:7

3. What should I include in my testimony about the Lord?

Read Acts 17:5; 18:7; 21:8; 12:12

4. What was one of the best tools early Christians used for evangelism?

Read Acts 5:17–41

5. In the midst of their persecution, what did an angel tell the apostles to do?

Read Acts 8:1–7, 26–40

6. What happened to the Jerusalem church? Results? Then what happened in Samaria?

7. How did God prepare for Philip's encounter with the Ethiopian?

afterword

If you've read this far, you know there are absolutes after all. In fact, you've studied eight of them. As you think back upon them, though, do you still wish that you had a reviewable list of do's and don'ts to guide your choices as you peer ahead into the twenty-first century?

No, you didn't find any possibility of that in this book. We warned you in the beginning that such was not the case. But what you did find is much more important.

These absolutes teach us to fill our hearts, minds, and lives with Christian concepts of right. As we do, wrongdoing stands out in abhorrence like a single rotten orange in a bowl of delectable fruit. To believe in God, to love, obey, and serve him is to commit ourselves to being and doing what he wants us to be and do. We are following his guidelines for living.

We've learned that we can anchor ourselves in truth and in God's love. From these eight beginning absolutes we find the basis from which to say yes or no to the choices we face every day. For example, if we believe in God and accept Jesus, his Son, as our

Savior, we can turn to him for aid and answers. We can ask him not only for daily bread or help with difficulties, but we can also count on his leadership and his caring when we're confused or tempted.

In Matthew 23, Jesus talked to the Jewish leaders about their perpetual preoccupation with religious legalisms instead of with living righteous, loving lives. He put it simply enough in verse 26 so that none of us can miss his meaning:

"First clean the inside of the cup and dish," he said, "and then the outside also will be clean."

If you have committed yourself to the biblical absolutes you've just finished studying, the Holy Spirit has cleansed you inside. So, according to Jesus' comment to the Pharisees, he has cleaned up the exterior of your life as well, the things people see.

But the issues of life remain. Questions loom. Shall I? Or shall I not? May I? Must I?

When you face such questions, you must apply on your own the principles you've used through these pages. Search your Bible. Read it with your ears and heart open to the Holy Spirit's teaching. You know that he is with you to help you understand the concepts that apply to your questions.

Some answers will come through loudly and clearly. Yes, you may. No, you mustn't. Others will be less open and blunt but will probe your motivation, the reasons that underlie your asking, and the desires that mold your choices. The Holy Spirit will also help you to understand the ways those desires either align themselves with the Lord's wishes for you or delude you into pursuing self-gratifying plans.

God himself is the divine Absolute, the Creator

and Giver of life to whom the whole world is deeply, dearly beloved. Jesus reveals to us God's heart of love and his plans and purposes for us. The Bible tells us what we can be if we obey him, if we embrace its absolutes. If you have decided to trust, obey, love, and serve him; to search his Book and listen to the voice of the Holy Spirit, the completion of this study of absolutes has become the beginning of your life upon the Way.